GOD'S HARVEST

God Bless you

Arthur W Dodds

2 COR 5 ^{19} LB

GOD'S HARVEST

BY

Arthur Dodds

Dianthus Publishing Limited

Published by Dianthus Publishing Ltd,
The Pool House, Kemble
Cirencester. GL7 6AD
Tel. 01285 770 239 · Fax: 01285 770 896
E-mail: cbrann@dianthus.prestel.co.uk

Copy Sales: The Secretary, Harnhill Manor,
Cirencester, Glos, GL7 5PX
Tel: 01285 850283/4 Fax: 01285850519

E-mail: office@harnhillcentre.freeserve.co.uk
Website: www.harnhillcentre.freeserve.co.uk

© Canon Arthur Dodds, AD 2000,   Printed in England

ISBN 0-946604 -18-5   **Price per copy: £5.90**

Illustrations:

Chapter	Title	Page

Harnhill Manor, which became the Harnhill Centre

Jennifer Rees Larcombe

I've been reading the manuscript of this book while I've been staying here at Harnhill, on a private retreat. I arrived feeling a bit battered by life and totally drained but as I drove over the cattle grid and up the drive the same thing happened, just as it always does! I felt like a small, vulnerable chick running for cover under the soft, protecting wings of a large mother hen. Harnhill always makes me feel safe like that, and I guess many others share the experience because this place is far more than just a honey coloured manor house in the Cotswolds. It is a safe place; a refuge to which people can come to be mended in body, soul and mind.

This book is written by the man to whom God entrusted the tiny seed of vision which became Harnhill. His first book told us how that seed began to grow, and I expected his second book to continue the story, bringing us up to date with tales of how the draughty old barn was transformed into a beautiful conference suite; how a dining room was built where chickens used to run and the dairy became a Counselling Centre. I thought I would read about financial needs being met miraculously and how prayers were answered for planning permission. But Arthur only touches briefly on all that; to him Harnhill is about people, not about buildings, finances and slick organisation. So he introduces us to some of the people who came here because they were facing a crisis in their lives; a gaping loss; a marriage breakdown; a grim diagnosis or a sense of having lost God under the sheer junk of modern life. People like them come to Harnhill day after day, week after week in search of restoration – restoration with God, themselves and with others. He brings their stories to life, simply because he writes about them with such interest and compassion. I found 'meeting' them deeply encouraging and inspiring because what happened to them shows so clearly that God is still in the restoration business today.

But Arthur does not only tell us the stories of people. There is another strand running through this book. It gripped me so powerfully I found myself easing my feet out of my shoes because I felt I was on Holy Ground. Woven in among the stories of people, Arthur also tells us God's story. In a gentle but masterly way he takes us through the Bible, explaining God's unfolding plan for the restoration of mankind; lifting it right off the dusty academic shelf, where so many theologians hide it, and making it real, relevant and alive for people living in the twenty-first century.

Most of us, at some time in our lives, ask the question, 'Why does God allow His special friends to go through times of pain and suffering?' It is hard for those of us who love and respect Arthur to see him struggling with illness and debilitating weakness, when he loves travelling the country telling people about God's desire and ability to heal and restore broken lives. Yet it was simply because his illness made travelling and preaching impossible that this book was written. Arthur is sure God distinctly told him to write a book saying all the things he would talk about if he were able to accept his many invitations to speak and minister healing.

As I finally finished the manuscript I felt Arthur was handing on to all of us his own personal 'Treasures of Darkness' (Isaiah 45.3). I found this book compulsive reading, and I believe it will not only fascinate anyone who has ever been to Harnhill but will also be of great interest to those who have not been here – yet!

Jennifer Rees Larcombe

November 2000

Since the publication of Desert Harvest in 1993 various people have asked me, "When are you going to write another book?" I have replied, "I'm not!"
Two years ago I became ill with repeated chest infections which affected my heart. I had to cancel all speaking engagements and decline others. A year ago as I was dragging myself around a few steps at a time I said to God "What use am I to you like this?" The reply came, "Write another book!" He continued "Include in it much of the material you use when you do accept speaking engagements."

Within a month, my wife Letty tripped in the hall and broke her thigh. Five weeks later she came out of hospital even more lame and immobile than she had been previously. As a result, what little energy I could muster had to be used to cook and look after her.

In April 2000 two friends, Penelope Bourdillon and Marcia Gibson-Watt came to a week's course at the Harnhill Centre. They came to our cottage nearby to see us. On learning the situation Penelope immediately said in her pro-active way "You must come and stay with us. I will look after Letty and provide meals while you write." She continued, "I know I shall be at home the last part of May to get the garden ready for opening; come then!" By courtesy of son-in-law David driving us we spent a very enjoyable ten days with Penelope and Mervyn at Llwyn Madoc, not far from Builth Wells.

On the last night Penelope drove us over to a gathering of Christians at the home of Marcia and Robin Gibson-Watt not far away. At the end of the evening Marcia asked me how the book was progressing. "I'm about half way through," I replied. "Then you must come here at the beginning of August and finish it." We did. I am deeply indebted to both homes for providing such excellent facilities for me to be able to write. Also to Marcia, an accomplished artist, for the painting of the Harnhill Barn which is on the cover of the book.

I am also very grateful to various other people: to Jeremy Wellesley-Baldwin for transforming my longhand scrawl into something legible and through computer wizardry sending it by e-mail to the Harnhill office. To Mary Sanders for receiving it there and making various corrections and additions to the disc ready for the publisher. To Jennifer Rees Larcombe for honouring me with a generous Foreword. To Christian Brann for again eagerly agreeing to publish and doing it so quickly. And to many other people who have contributed in one way or another, especially those who have let me use their personal stories of healing.

Finally I thank God for His continuing love and bringing once again something out of my weakness and sickness that hopefully may be of use to others.

As Malcolm Muggeridge has said, "I have known more of God in times of struggle and suffering than in times of brightness and light."

Arthur Dodds

Harnhill, November 2000

In the Beginning God

On November 6th 1999 the large barn at Harnhill, which had been beautifully restored and re-ordered, was officially opened, blessed and dedicated by the Right Reverend John Perry, Bishop of Chelmsford. He and his wife Gay have been very supportive of the Harnhill Centre of Christian Healing from its beginning in 1986.

As I sat there during the ceremony, thoughts which had often been at the back of my mind came forcibly to the front. I pictured the beautifully large barn in former days at harvest time when mountains of grain poured into it and the whole place was a bustle of activity. Now it was full again, and is frequently full, of people as they pour in for the healing services, training days and conferences.

Then they go out again to the various parts of the country from which they have come, and occasionally from abroad, to share their good news. Some go out newly restored in body, mind, emotions and spirit. This process goes on week after week, not just once a year as with the old harvest. The Barn is now a focus for a different sort of harvest: God's harvest of restored lives. As John Mockett, the Deputy Warden said one night when preaching at a healing service, "We are in the restoration business. God's restoration business."

"For God was in Christ restoring the world to himself .... This is the wonderful message He has given us to tell others" (2 Cor. 5v19 Living Bible). Verse 21 continues "For God took the sinless Christ and poured into Him our sins. Then, in exchange, He poured God's goodness into us." What a wonderful process in which to be involved, as we are at Harnhill day in and day out.

One person who benefited from this process at Harnhill was Tessa. She states:

"By a series of wonderful God-incidents, I was brought into contact with the Harnhill Centre of Christian Healing and so began a process of restoration."

Tessa writes: "The person I am today and am continuing to become (my new creation!) is so immeasurably different from the quivering, emotional wreck who was first taken to Harnhill in 1992. Years of childhood abuse – emotional, physical, mental, sexual – had reduced me to a pitiful state of being in which I truly believed – as I had been brought up to believe – that I was the lowest of the low, the scum of the earth, a vile, useless, unlovable lump of nothingness. At first I was shocked to think that the likes of me could be acceptable and accepted in such a place, but gradually the love – the unconditional, non-judgmental love that permeates Harnhill – broke through the seemingly impenetrable wall within which I had encased myself."

"It was with great trepidation that I presented myself at Harnhill for my first week's stay for counselling and prayer ministry. I simply had no concept of what lay before me in the coming week. All I knew was that I hurt in a way I couldn't begin to explain or even acknowledge to myself. What I encountered was love and compassion such as I had never experienced before and an unqualified acceptance of me, complete with all my 'warts' and 'blemishes'. Much of the time I was scarcely able to speak during my first session as I was so filled with shame and humiliation but my counsellors were so very gentle and kind and their prayers so heartfelt and sincere that I gradually began to relax a little and for the first time in my life I found I was able to begin to tell someone (virtual strangers, at that!) a little of the traumas that had brought me, so burdened, broken and wounded to their door."

"So many areas were touched upon during that week – my enforced exposure to the occult as a child, the violence and abuse of my home life – and I began to learn about true forgiveness. I re-committed my life to the Lord Jesus in a more meaningful way and determined to 'work out my healing' when I returned home.

I received so many blessings that week and was released from so much of my pain and fear, that by the time I left to go back to my family, I truly believed that I was healed, once and for all, free at last! Little did I realise at the time that the journey had only just begun!"

Tessa continues to come to Harnhill from time to time as the restoration process continues and the Holy Spirit transforms her into Christ's likeness "with ever increasing glory," (2 Cor. 3.v18). She also comes to help at the Centre.

"In the beginning God created the heavens and the earth" (Gen. 1v1) He created them in great beauty and harmony. Everything was perfect "And God saw everything that He had made, and behold it was very good" (Gen. 1v31). At the peak of this creation "God created man in his own image, ... male and female created He them" (Gen.1v27). God placed them in a perfect garden, the Garden of Eden, and He told them to be fruitful and multiply; "And God gave them dominion over the fish of the sea, and over the birds of the air, and over the cattle, and over all the earth" (Gen. 1v26). And God told them to look after the garden and enjoy it and to eat of the fruit of the trees of the garden except for the Tree of Life in the middle of the garden; that they must not touch for fear of death.

Into this idyllic situation enters Satan in the guise of a serpent. He sidles up to the woman and, as he still does, begins his temptation by sowing doubt of God's word in Eve's mind with a half-truth: "Did God really say you must not eat of any tree in the garden?" (Gen. 3v1). Eve corrected the serpent, saying that God had permitted them to eat any of the fruit except that of the tree in the middle of the garden: "You must not touch it or you will surely die." But doubt had been sown in

Eve's mind and Satan is quick to follow up with a deliberate lie: "You will not surely die for God knows when you eat of it, your eyes will be opened and you will be like God, knowing good from evil." (Gen. 3v4 & 5) Eve is confused and vulnerable and flattered and falls for Satan's plan. "When the woman saw that the fruit of the tree was good and pleasing to the eye and also desirable for giving wisdom she took some and ate it. She also gave some to her husband."

Satan still operates in much the same way with us. For Adam and Eve that first act of disobedience was literally fatal as God had warned. It brought separation from God and so spiritual death, both for themselves and for mankind. They were expelled from the garden as no longer fit to tend it and enjoy its blessings. Through their disobedience, sin, death, disease, disorder, disruption and discord entered the world of beauty and harmony. Further by obeying Satan rather God, Satan was able to usurp the dominion of the earth that God granted to Adam and Eve. And the more mankind sinned and obeyed Satan in succeeding generations the greater the chaos as Satan gained more and more control of the world. By the time Jesus came, He three times called Satan "The ruler of the world", e.g. John 16v11. Satan happily agreed with this title and in the Temptations showed Jesus in an instant all the kingdoms of the world, and he said "I will give you all this authority and splendour, for it has been given to me and I can give it to anyone I want to. So if you worship me it will be yours" (Luke 4v5-7).

Such was the enormity of Adam and Eve's first disobedience. Their fall from grace broke four all-important relationships. It broke the relationship between man and God, Adam and Eve had had an easy and full fellowship with God until their disobedience. But now when God came to walk in the garden in the cool of the day they hid themselves (Gen. 3v8). They chose to separate themselves from the Lord God. That is what sin does: separates us from God.

The second relationship that was broken was between each other, man and his fellow. When God called out to them and asked why they were hiding, Adam blamed Eve for giving him the fruit of the forbidden tree; the first of many such occasions of husbands blaming their wives; the first of many domestic quarrels. Worse was to follow in the next generation: man murdering his brother.

The third relationship that was broken was that of man with himself. They experienced guilt in place of peace of mind. They were ashamed of themselves, ashamed of being naked. Guilt, shame and lack of peace of mind is still a consequence of sin.

The fourth relationship that was broken was between man and his environment. In the Garden of Eden man and woman and their environment were in perfect harmony, but their disobedience had made them unworthy of stewarding such a perfect place. Expulsion from the garden meant painful toil among thorns and thistles: "Only by the sweat of their brow .... " would they now eat food (Gen. 3v18,19).

Many who come to Harnhill for help have experienced the pain of more than one of those broken relationships, as with Tessa above. Sometimes they have suffered the effects of all four of those broken relationships and are in need of restoration and healing.

The disobedience of Adam and Eve continued in succeeding generations. The more men and women sinned, the more dominion and control Satan obtained, with a resultant increase of disorder, disease, disruption, disaster and disharmony. As chaos increased, so the plight of men and women became more and more desperate. What did God do? Did God wash His hands of the whole situation? Did He say: "They have brought this upon themselves, let them get out of it by themselves if they can." No! Fortunately for all of us God is infinite love: "He so loved the world that he gave ...." He put into effect a contingency plan for mankind's restoration; a very costly rescue operation. It began with calling out a people who would seek to obey

Him and love Him and worship Him.

"The Lord God saw how great man's wickedness on earth had become" (Gen. 6v4) "But Noah found favour in the eyes of the Lord" (Gen. 6v8). Not only was Noah a righteous man, but an incredibly obedient man as he and his family built the ark according to God's specifications amidst the laughter and scorn of their neighbours. But through their obedience God was able to rescue them from the destruction of the wicked world and give them and the animal kingdom a new start sealed by a covenant symbolised by the rainbow.

However it was not long before man's desire to have the power of God re-appeared and the people began to build a tower that would reach to the heavens, the Tower of Babel. But they fell into disunity (broken relationships again), and ceased to build and were scattered.

God sought out again from the sinful world a man of faith and obedience who would be the father of a nation of faith through whom God could work out his purposes of salvation. He called out Abraham from the city of Ur to go and start a new people: "And Abraham went out, not knowing where he was to go" (Heb. 11v8). Eventually he was led to the land of Canaan and in his old age Isaac was born to Sarah. A further test followed when Abraham had to be willing to sacrifice his only son to demonstrate his faith in and obedience to, God. Isaac survived and the blessing is passed on to his son Jacob, whose character and name is changed when he wrestles one night with God at Peniel. Jacob had first had to marry Leah before he was later to marry the beautiful Rachel and it was some time before a son was born to Rachel, the colourful Joseph. He was the next instrument God used to save His people from starvation by bringing Joseph to leadership and his people to Egypt. However, later a Pharaoh arose in Egypt who did not know about Joseph the Israelite. Pharaoh was alarmed at the great rate of increase in their population and laid on the Israelites hard bondage and slavery.

God again comes to the rescue calling Moses as His instrument as he was tending his father-in-law's sheep in the desert by Mount Horeb. The story of the burning bush through which God spoke and called Moses is well known. To some this story may seem strange or far-fetched, but it continues to be so when God calls people to His service. His choosing of people (and of places), may seem strange, but God knows what He is about. He spoke to John Bunyan and Fred Lemon and others in a prison cell, to Saul on the Damascus road and to me in a burning bush in the desert but not for such an awesome task as Moses.

I had been shot down in the Western Desert in World War II and was seeking to tramp back over 120 miles of desert to Allied lines. I lay one day under a bush as the only shelter visible for hundreds of miles. The desert bush had no leaves but vicious spikes; and I had to crawl under it as the sun rose. It was no real shelter from the sun, but it was from the prying eyes of the enemy as I discovered later when a German truck stopped not far from me. An officer got out and surveyed the landscape through his binoculars but saw nothing in the thorn bush. I slept the sleep of extreme exhaustion until about midday when I awoke refreshed, conscious of nothing but the sun and blue sky above me and miles and miles of desert around me. I was alone, totally alone with God. And He spoke and said: "Why are you running away from me? You know I have been calling you to be my minister for some time." I mumbled a response to the effect that I was not good enough, my academic standard was inadequate (owing to all my illnesses) and I could never stand up before people and preach. He cut in before I could continue my excuses and said: "I will give you strength for anything I want you to do ." I could not find a reply to that and so tamely replied: "Alright, but it will have to be up to you, I cannot do it. But I promise that when I get back I will send my name in for consideration for ordination." This I did a few months later from prisoner-of-war camp.

When God calls, there needs to be a response, even if only a rather lame one like mine. I remember a missionary doctor on furlough from Africa some years ago telling how he trekked many miles into the jungle to hold a clinic there every two or three months in a remote part. One time when he arrived there the local chief had built a clinic and small hospital and proudly showed the doctor it: "Now we can have our own doctor" he said. The missionary replied that it might not be that easy. But, said the chief: "You have plenty of doctors in Britain. Will not God call one of them to come here?" The missionary replied: "He does call but people do not always respond to the call." Someone has said: "When man listens, God speaks; when man obeys, God acts." Miracles often result and His purposes are fulfilled.

Moses' response may have been a little tentative, but he had responded and he did obey and God was able to use him mightily through many signs and wonders to lead His people out of slavery toward the promised land. Moses was obedient, enabling God to work His wonders like dividing the Red Sea, but people were not always obedient and sometimes complaining. They had to endure a great deal of wandering and purging and agree to the covenant based on the Ten Commandments before they were fit to enter the promised land and then not under Moses, but under God's next chosen leader Joshua. Moses was able to look into the promised land from Mount Nebo and saw the green of it but then handed over to Joshua and died.

In the last three parties I led to the Holy Land I always went to Jordan first. Petra is a fascinating place. Whether David ever got there I don't know, but when in the psalms he speaks of God as a rock fortress, totally secure, my mind always pictures Petra. But the real highlight for me in Jordan was to stand where Moses stood, on Mount Nebo, looking into the Holy Land. You can see Jericho clearly with its palms and abundance of citrus fruits and on a very clear day it is possible to see Jerusalem. One could imagine Moses' delight at the view after all his hardships; his God-given task was accomplished. But for me what was even more striking was to look back over the mile upon mile of inhospitable desert hills and valleys over which Moses had led that great multitude of God's people. An impossible task without God's constant help, which now Joshua needed and which God promised him: "As I was with Moses so I will be with you .... Be strong and courageous because you will lead these people to inherit the land" (Joshua. 1v5-6). With God's help they crossed the River Jordan. With God's help as they obeyed His instructions, the walls of Jericho fell down and they went up and possessed the city. So gradually they settled into the promised land, each tribe in his allocated territory. As long as they obeyed and worshipped the God of Abraham, Isaac and Jacob, they prospered.

King David enlarged and secured their boundaries. King Solomon built a magnificent temple as a focus of their worship and as a witness of God's presence in their midst. But it was not long before they were enticed by the pagans among whom they lived, to try out their immoral practices and worship their gods. God raised up prophet after prophet who thundered against such practices and against the leaders who exploited the poor while living in luxury themselves. Such great men as Elijah and Elisha warned the people of Israel that such practices would inevitably lead to destruction and exile. Yet even Amos, who was most vehement in his condemnation of their disobedience of God's laws still held out hope if they would repent. God will still work out His purposes of redemption through a faithful remnant after the purging and destruction: "I will restore the fortunes of my people Israel, and they shall rebuild the ruined cities and inhabit them. They shall plant vineyards and drink their wine, and they shall make gardens and eat their fruit" (Amos. 9v14).

The great prophets Isaiah, Jeremiah and Ezekiel gained further insight into God's way of salvation. Dependence for God's favour on the outward building of a temple in their midst was a sham unless His presence was also within the temple of each individual heart. Similarly with outward knowledge of the Law, unless it was known within each person and practised. The day would come, God proclaimed through Jeremiah: ".... when I will make a new covenant with the house of Israel and with the house of Judah .... I will put my law in their minds and write it on their hearts ...." (Jeremiah. 3v31.33).

Further, Isaiah saw that men were unable to be obedient and keep the law, unable to love and worship the Lord their God by their own effort. They needed extra and powerful help from Him to do so; they needed a saviour, a redeemer whom God promised Isaiah to give: "For to us a child is born, to us a son is given, and the government will be on his shoulders and he will be called Wonderful Counsellor, Mighty God, Everlasting Father, Prince of Peace" (Is. 9v6).

Not a mighty warrior saviour, but a servant king who would bear men's sorrows and heal their diseases and take upon himself the consequences of their sins (Is. 53). And even when that was achieved the prophet Joel foresaw that powerful help, divine help, would continue to be needed and prophesied that the empowering of the Holy Spirit of God would be available to all: "And afterwards I will pour out my spirit on all people." (Joel. 2v28).

Truly, as John White wrote in The Shattered Mirror: "The Old Testament represents the slow unfolding of God's plan to provide the means of our redemption."

Jesus

When the time was right or as Paul puts it: "When the fullness of time was come ....," the crucial phase of God's costly rescue operation took place. A tiny, fragile, vulnerable baby was born to a teenage mother, not in a great palace, but in a grubby eastern stable in a small enemy-occupied country, in the town of Bethlehem, fulfilling Micah's prophecy (Micah. 5v2). God breaks into human history in the most humble of circumstances and becomes part of His own creation. He chose to start at the very bottom of the pile of the human race. Laying aside the glory and status that is His by right, He identifies with the lowest of mankind (Phil. 2v6). Even so He is welcomed, not only by shepherds, but by wise, princely astronomers from the east. Instantly His life is put under threat from King Herod which causes Joseph to flee to Egypt as a refugee. Only when King Herod has died in a rather gruesome way are they able to return to the small hill town of Nazareth in Galilee to re-establish the family carpentry business. Jesus grows up there, going to school in the local synagogue like other Jewish boys learning the scriptures, and from Joseph the craft of carpentry.

When Jesus was aged 12 years, the age for Bar Mitzvah, He went to Jerusalem and in the Temple gave a glimpse of His future ability as a debater. He also showed an awareness of a special relationship with His Heavenly Father, though still subject to His human parents (Luke. 2v51).

When the time was right and Jesus was nearly 30 years old, he associated himself with the renewal movement that was taking place through His cousin John the Baptist. In spite of John's protests Jesus was baptised in the River Jordan. As He was coming out of the water the Holy Spirit descended on Him like a dove and a voice from Heaven declared: "You are my beloved Son in whom I am well pleased." Then the Holy Spirit immediately drove Him out into the wilderness to be tempted by Satan. The devil recognised the threat the impending Ministry of Jesus would be to him, described by John later: "The reason the Son of God appeared was to destroy the works of the devil" (1 John. 3v8). In John's Gospel we have the other side of the coin, the positive side: "God so loved the world that He gave his only son that whoever believes in Him should not perish but have eternal life" (John. 3v16).

Jesus confronts the very real temptations of Satan and rebuffs each with a word of scripture. The temptation to win people to God's Kingdom by miraculously providing for their material needs. Stones into bread. Winning people by miraculous stunts in throwing himself off the

THIS IS MY BELOVED SON WITH WHOM I AM WELL PLEASED

Jesus' Baptism
Woodcut by Peter Kent

pinnacle of the Temple and landing safely; or winning the world by compromising by "making a deal" with the ruler of this world. Rejecting these temptations enabled Jesus to be clear that rescuing mankind could only be achieved by sacrificial love.

Mark's account goes on to tell of Jesus beginning to collect a team around Him, initially of Galilean fishermen. On the Sabbath He goes into the synagogue at Caperneum to teach with authority and drives out an unclean spirit from one of the congregation, indicating that the clash with Satan continues. Afterwards they go next door to Peter's mother-in-law's house. She is sick in bed with a high fever. Jesus takes her by the hand and heals her and she gets up and prepares a meal for Jesus and His disciples. By the time they have finished a huge crowd has gathered outside the door bringing all their sick. He heals them of their various diseases and casts out demons from any possessed. Next morning before dawn Jesus gets up and goes out to a lonely place to pray. Some time later the disciples find Him and say that many people are looking for Him, but He replies He must go into other villages and preach there.

Right at the beginning of His ministry we see how the clash with Satan continues with Jesus casting out evil spirits. We also notice how important to him are times of prayer. This pattern continues throughout His ministry. Later, for instance, He spends a whole night in prayer before choosing His twelve disciples. He needs the prayer to discern the Father's will; here, it is to go to other villages to preach there also. John's Gospel says: "He can do only what He sees the father doing" (John. 5v19). He also needs times of prayer for the continuing empowering of His Ministry by the Holy Spirit. After the exhausting Sabbath at Capernaeum, instead of having a lie-in the next morning: "While it is still dark .... He went off to a solitary place, where He prayed." We have a similar incident in Luke's Gospel when crowds of people came to hear Him and be healed of their diseases and He withdrew to a lonely place for prayer. Then in the next verse we read: "the power of the Lord was present for Him to heal the sick" (Luke 5v17). The word power there in the Greek is 'dunamis' our word 'dynamite'. In the next verse He heals a paralytic man.

From the very beginning of the concept of the Harnhill Centre of Christian Healing, eighteen months before the Centre opened, we were convinced of the all-importance of prayer. It began in the little church next to the Manor with a few of us at 7 am on a Tuesday morning for one hour. Further periods were soon added and sometimes we had a whole night vigil of prayer. Once the Centre was opened and running, prayer continued to be a priority, mainly for the same two reasons as in Jesus' s Ministry; the discerning of the Father's will for all aspects of the developing centre and for the constant empowering of the Holy Spirit.

Those who come to the Centre today continue to find its life based on prayer and often themselves come to receive prayer. Sue writes: "About six years ago I explored the possibility that God was calling me to ordination. As an ordinand, with all the crises which come with it, I often found myself at the Centre or with Arthur and Letty and it was there that I found the safety and security of God. They helped me discern God's call and also helped me to see what was important in faith and those things that needed to be sorted out. A couple of times during essay crises and often before I was to take services, I attended worship at Harnhill and received prayer for these things."

"As ordination approached I wanted to go somewhere where I felt completely safe and secure and I spent a couple of days at the Centre surrounded by the care and love of God's people who sent me on my way with prayer. There was nothing dramatic but a calm reassurance of the shelter, safety and touch of God."

Sue adds: "Harnhill is a place of peace, restoration, prayer and reassurance of God's love."

Early in His Ministry Jesus returns in the "Power of the Spirit" to His home town of Nazareth. On the Sabbath He went into the synagogue "as was His custom." The scroll of the prophet Isaiah was handed to Him and He read "the Spirit of the Lord is upon me, because He has anointed me to preach the good news to the poor. He has sent me to proclaim release to the captives and the recovery of sight to the blind, to set at liberty those who are oppressed" (Luke. 4v18).

This prophecy of Isaiah was like a job description to Jesus for His Ministry. The Spirit's anointing for that ministry He had received at His baptism and continued to receive through His frequent times of prayer enabling Him to fulfil the rest of the prophecy: "To preach the good news to the poor". The poor feature prominently in His life and teaching as in the Sermon on the Mount and parables. The poor were dear to His compassionate heart, for in the culture of His day they were ignored, deprived and rejected. Their poverty was seen by some Jewish leaders to be an indication that they were sinners, disapproved of by God. The sick were similarly regarded. Jesus seeks to reverse this concept and show that they are precious to God. He preaches good news to them rather than the condemnation of doom they were used to hearing. The Greek word translated 'good news' is 'euangelios' from which we get the word evangelism. It is right for us Christians to remind ourselves constantly that our message is GOOD news. I once heard David Pawson speaking about this word. He described a Roman special messenger being sent back from one of the far-flung frontiers of the Empire where a battle was in progress. The messenger ran or rode the first stage and then passed it on to another messenger to take it on the next stage and so on all the way back to Rome where the final messenger burst into the Senate crying: "euangelios, euangelios!" (good news, good news – Victory!). This conveys the importance, the urgency and the sense of victory of the Christian message: Good News, a far cry from the gloom and doom preached in some of our churches. This accounts in part for the reluctance of our present poor to turn for help to the church. In Philip Yancey's book "What's So Amazing About Grace?" the drug addict prostitute says, when it is suggested she go to church for help: "Why should I ever go there? I am already feeling terrible about myself, they'll just make me feel worse."

One of the reactions of the poor and needy who come to the Harnhill Centre is that of great surprise at the unconditional, non-judgmental welcome; the way in which they are immediately received in love and acceptance as Tessa described in Chapter 1.

The good news of Jesus is precious especially to the poor and needy. He preaches good news, but also demonstrates it in practice in his compassionate ministry of healing the sick, casting out demons, feeding the hungry, stilling the storm and raising the dead.

The job description in Luke 4 goes on to say: "He sent me to proclaim release to the captives", not least those in captivity to sin. As the angel told Joseph before the birth of Jesus: "You shall call His name Jesus, for He will save His people from their sins" (Matt. 1v21).

The quotation from Isaiah 61 goes on: "The recovering of sight to the blind," Jesus did indeed heal the blind including the man born blind in John 9 and the blind beggar Bartimeus in Jericho. There were others. And Jesus was equally concerned with the spiritually blind, and we still get plenty of those coming to Harnhill for healing.

Jesus is concerned to heal all sickness, physical, spiritual and mental. The Greek word for healing by the gospel writers is "sozo" which can also be translated as "save". It's the root word for salvation. The desire of Jesus for us all is total and eternal salvation. Physical healing is good, but Jesus wants our wholeness, whole salvation. The woman with the issue of blood for twelve years who pushed her way through the crowd to touch the hem of the garment Jesus was wearing immediately received healing for the haemorrhage. That was not enough for Jesus who turned and said: "Who touched me?" When the woman threw herself at Jesus' feet and confessed all, that put her into a new relationship with God and Jesus was able then to say: "Go your way; your faith has made you whole .... saved you".

Similarly with the lepers. All ten were cleansed as they obeyed Jesus and went on their way to report to the priests. But the one who returned and threw himself at the feet of Jesus to give thanks to God received the further blessing as Jesus declared: "Go your way; your faith has saved you – made you whole"

When John the Baptist was languishing in prison he wanted assurance that Jesus was indeed the Messiah. So he sent two of his disciples to ask Jesus "Are you he who is to come, or shall we look for another?" (Luke. 7v20). The Gospel record continues: "In that hour He cured many of diseases and plagues and evil spirits and on many who were blind He bestowed sight. And He answered them: 'Go and tell John what you have seen and heard.' The blind received their sight, the lame walk, lepers are cleansed and the deaf hear, the dead are raised up and the poor have the good news preached to them." This was a clear confirmation that Jesus is the Messiah. The Kingdom of God and the King were present.

"To set at liberty those who are oppressed," Isaiah had prophesied as Jesus had read out in the synagogue at Nazareth. It has already been noted how frequently Jesus cast out demons to set at liberty those who were oppressed. This continued clash with Satan is focused in all three synoptic gospels in the story of Beelzebub. Jesus cast out a dumb spirit and in Matthew it is the Pharisees who said: "He casts out demons by Beelzebub, the prince of demons." Jesus points out that such an argument is illogical: "How can Satan cast out Satan?" He asks, "If a kingdom is divided against itself, that kingdom cannot stand." (Mark. 3v24) "But if it's by the finger ("spirit" in Mark) of God that I cast out demons, the Kingdom of God has come upon you" (Luke. 11v20).

The Kingdom of God is the main theme of the teachings of Jesus. Most of His parables begin "the Kingdom of God is like ...." and then illustrate some truth about the Kingdom. Basically God's Kingdom is where He rules. As Jesus tells us to pray: "Your Kingdom come, Your will be done on earth as in heaven;" His Kingdom is where His will is done. And the sermon on the mount speaks out the kind of life lived in God's Kingdom. This teaching of Jesus is demonstrated in His life of sacrificial love, in His signs and wonders and in His uncompromising opposition to evil. His Kingdom is totally opposed to Satan. The longer His Ministry goes on, the stronger the opposition gets, leading towards an inevitable climax. The opposition may seem to come from surprising quarters like the religious leaders of the day but it is all initiated and orchestrated by Satan. Even Peter on one occasion receives the rebuke from Jesus: "Get behind me Satan." (Mark. 8v33).

As the opposition increased, Jesus occasionally withdrew to territories outside Jewish jurisdiction; to the region of Tyre and Sidon, to the ten towns of Decapolis and the villages of Caesarea Philippi. Away from the Jewish opposition, Jesus was able to spend more time teaching His disciples and preparing them for the future. It was in the area of Caesarea Philippi that He asked them: "Who do men say that I am?" When they gave the answer: "Some say John the Baptist, others Elijah or one of the prophets" Jesus asked them: "But who do you say that I am?" Peter answered, "You are the Christ" (Mark. 8v29). From that time Jesus began to warn them that He must suffer many things, be rejected and killed, and after three days rise again. But they did not understand. A week later Jesus takes Peter, James and John up a mountain to pray. There He is transfigured before them and they see Him in something of his true splendour and glory and He is seen conferring with Moses and Elijah, representing God's Law and the prophets, whom Jesus is fulfilling. It is confirmation of the status of Jesus which Peter had recognised a week earlier. Coming down to the harsh realities of the world, Jesus heals an epileptic that the other disciples had been unable to help and He urges them to have more prayer and faith. He warns them again of his coming death and "set His face to go up to Jerusalem" (Luke. 9v30).

In Mark's gospel there is a sense of urgency about Christ's Ministry conveyed by His frequent use of the word "immediately." Immediately Jesus moves from one event to the next. John's gospel however is firmly set in a long term eternal dimension; "In the beginning was the Word .... He came to His own and His own received Him not." Events move in the fore-ordained pace of God. Jesus can wait a further two days after hearing the disturbing news from Martha and Mary that His dear friend Lazarus is very ill. This turns out to be for the greater glory of God when Lazarus is raised and Jesus is able to demonstrate as well as say "I am the resurrection and the life."

Mark's urgency and John's calm unhurriedness are both features of Christ's Ministry and should be of ours. As Jesus moves steadily yet urgently towards Jerusalem and the climax of His Mission, bringing as He passes, new life to Zechariah and sight to the blind Bartimeus, Satan seems to get more frantic. Time and again he has failed to tempt Jesus or divert Him from His rescuing, restoring, healing activity. Now Satan seeks to mobilise all the evil in men and women through the ages to heap upon Jesus in an attempt to break his trusting obedient relationship with the Father. The battle is fierce in this last week. Jesus quietly and purposefully goes forward. He rides into Jerusalem, not on a war-horse, but humbly on the donkey of Zechariah (Zech. 9v9). He allows the people at last to have their desire to proclaim Him Messiah, casting garments in His path and waving palm branches of victory. But when He enters the city whose name means peace, He turns not to the right to confront the Roman garrison as the people had hoped, but He turns to the left to enter and cleanse the Temple of those who have made it a den of robbers rather than a house of prayer. Renewal must always start with the household of God.

During the week the enemy forces are mustered by Satan from among the Jewish leaders, the Roman authorities, the Herodians and ordinary people. They are all frenetic in their evil plotting and scheming. Jesus alone is calm as He fulfils His destiny. He gives the supreme example of the Servant King as He washes the disciples' feet, teaching them how to love each other. He makes careful provision for them to be able to abide in Him when He is gone, by breaking the bread and sharing the wine. And then more prayer. Surely in the history of mankind there have not been three hours of such intense prayer as that by Jesus in Gethsemane? Even today to go to that place is deeply moving. "With His soul deeply troubled and sorrowful unto death He went forward a few paces from the others and threw Himself on a large flat slab of rock and prayed: 'Abba, Father, all things are possible for you; remove this cup from me; yet not what I will, but what you will' (Mark. 14v34)." He repeated the prayer ever more fervently causing Him in His agony to sweat great drops of blood, Doctor Luke tells us. One wonders if the devil tempted Him by suggesting He could get out of it all by shinning over the garden wall and returning to His carpentry at Nazareth. If Satan did so tempt, it had no effect on Jesus who was set on doing His Father's will and completing the task set for Him. But if there was another way to fulfil God's purpose that would be welcome. After three hours of agonising prayer He knows He must go through with it and returns with resolution to the sleeping disciples and the traitor Judas with a band of the Temple Guards.

Then follows the mockery of a trial, everything illegally pushed through in haste during the night so that His death could be achieved before the Jewish festival. But their evil scheming only fulfils God's purpose. When the Passover lambs are being slaughtered the Lamb of God is dying on the Cross bearing the cost and consequences of the sins of all people. Even on the Cross the taunts and tests continue; "Come down from the cross and we will believe you." They still would not have believed and His Mission would then have been unfulfilled.

He continues to care and intercede for others to the end. For those crucifying Him He prays: "Father forgive them. They know not what they do." To the penitent thief He promises: "Today you will be with me in Paradise." He commits His mother and beloved disciples to each other: "behold your son – behold your mother" (John 18v2,27). His dehydration and great thirst He likened to His great thirst for humanity's salvation, which had brought Him to this hour and caused Him to cry out: "My God, My God why have you forsaken me?" Sin separates from God and in bearing mankind's sins Jesus is separated from His Father for the first and only time causing this most derelict of cries. No wonder there was darkness over the whole land. But still He cries out in the words of scripture: (Ps. 22) and shortly will be able to change the tone to one of victory: "It is finished," task accomplished, mission completed. And then thankfully: "Father, into your hands I commend my spirit" as He dies.

Satan gleefully heaped all mankind's evil sins on Jesus in an attempt to break Him but in doing so has helped to fulfil God's purpose for Jesus to bear the consequences of mens' sins that they might be free of them. His body is indeed broken, but not his spirit. The first Adam's disobedience which had led to the increasing chaos has now been reversed by the second Adam's total obedience, even unto death. A new start has begun. Christ's victory over sin and death and Satan is confirmed that first Easter morning when Jesus bursts forth from the tomb. It continues to be confirmed every time a Christian appropriates to himself or to herself Christ's forgiveness and new life.

The victory of Jesus on the cross and resurrection is the decisive battle in the great spiritual war in which we are all caught up. The war is not yet over but the triumphant end is now certain; Satan is a defeated foe.

It is a bit like a key victory by a school friend of mine who posthumously won the VC in the Burma campaign during the second World War. The Allied forces were pushing the Japanese back and retaking Burma. They were being held up by a key hill position overlooking the plains which was held by Japanese soldiers from which they could fire at the whole of that part of the Allied front. Two assaults had been made against the hill and repulsed with heavy losses. A third assault was launched led by my friend. As they attacked the position with great determination they again suffered heavy casualties as they went forward and upward. Men kept falling alongside him until only my friend was left still pressing on. Then he was severely wounded and fell to the ground. After a while he was able to continue to crawl painfully up the hill until he got near enough to lob hand grenades into the post and clear it of the enemy before he himself died of his wounds. Others were able to go up later in safety and claim the key post and the whole line was able to move forward. It was a key victory in the restoration of Burma.

Another analogy of what Jesus achieved is that of the Normandy landings in the second World War. Once the Allied forces had established a good bridgehead in France, Hitler's days were numbered. That key battle had been won at a heavy loss of life. Now more and more allied troops and armaments could be poured through that bridgehead to overrun the enemy-occupied territories. There would be further casualties in the advance as mopping-up operations continued, but final victory and the end of Hitler was assured. Jesus has won the decisive victory over Satan and his days are now numbered, he "knows his time is short" (Rev. 12v12). Ultimate and total triumph is assured but there will still be casualties as the Kingdom of God advances and the mopping-up operations continue in the winning back of enemy occupied territory. We, Christ's followers, have committed ourselves to the task of advancing His Kingdom and restoring the four broken relationships of the fall, something we cannot possibly do in our own strength, but we are not without the necessary help. Just as the Allies in their advance across Europe relied on replenishment of resources from the bridgehead so Jesus promises us unlimited resources through the Holy Spirit.

The enemy continues to be active and aggressive, maybe more so since he knows "his time is short." He has his agents through whom he speaks and acts. We see his activities in the hooligans and criminals who beat up and kill the very old for a few pounds or rape the very young. There are intellectuals too who speak for him like Frederick Nietsche, who in 1882 pronounced "God is dead," a cry that others have taken up since. Julian Huxley in 1957 wrote: "Operationally God is beginning to resemble not a ruler but the last fading smile of a cosmic Cheshire cat." The opposition from various quarters is strong towards the task to which Jesus has committed us, namely extending His Kingdom of restoration by love. It takes courage and dedication, but it is also one of the most exciting adventures there is in this life, suitable for the vigorous young like our grandson, Adam, reading theology at St Andrews, or our grand-daughter Sarah in her hard work with the disadvantaged in London through the Christian charity Besom, as well as for old fogies like my wife and myself.

For our leader and example we have one who was described by Peter, one of our many lay helpers, in a recent Wednesday evening healing service like this:

"He was born contrary to the laws of nature; Lived in obscurity;

He had no wealth or influence;

His relatives were inconspicuous and uninfluential.

In infancy He startled a king;

In boyhood He puzzled the doctors;

In manhood ruled the course of nature:

He walked upon the billows and hushed the sea to peace.

He healed the multitudes without medicine and made no charge for
   His services.

He never wrote a book, yet all the libraries in the land could not hold the books that have been written about Him.

He never wrote a song, yet He has furnished the theme of more songs than all the songwriters combined.

He never founded a college, yet all the schools cannot boast of as many students as He has.

He is the star of astronomy;

The rock of geology

The lion and Lamb of zoology;

The harmonizer of all discord and the healer of all diseases ....

Herod could not kill Him;

Satan could not seduce Him;

Death could not destroy Him;

The grave could not hold Him.

Great men have come and gone, yet He lives on.

I always think that the testimony of the Jewish historian Josephus is most striking. Born of a distinguished priestly family in Jerusalem in AD 37 his major work is "The Antiquity of the Jews" written in Greek and published in AD 93 in twenty volumes. In chapter three of book eighteen, writing of Pilate and his relations with the Jews, he says:

"Now there was about this time Jesus, a wise man, if it be lawful to call him a man, for he was a doer of wonderful works – a teacher of such men as receive the truth with pleasure. He drew over to him many of the Jews and many of the Gentiles. He was [the] Christ; and when Pilate, at the suggestion of the principal men among us, had condemned him to the cross, those that loved him at the first did not forsake him, for he appeared to them alive again the third day, as the divine prophets had foretold these and ten thousand other wonderful things concerning him and the tribe of Christians, named from him, are not extinct at this day."

Jesus lives on and His Kingdom expands through His Body, the Church, operating under the guidance and inspiration of the Holy Spirit.

God the Holy Spirit

During His life on earth Jesus told His disciples to carry on His Ministry when He had returned to Heaven. In fact the word disciple in the Aramaic can also mean apprentice: one who watches and works with the master craftsman until he or she is able to do the work the master craftsman does. Jesus says to His disciples: "The works I do you will do also and greater works than these will you do because I go to the Father;" "greater" not in quality but in quantity, because Jesus in his incarnate body was limited to one place at one time. Through His new body the Church He could operate in many places at the same time, through the enabling of His Holy Spirit.

While still with them Jesus gave His disciples a trial run, first the twelve in Luke 9v1,2: "Jesus called the twelve and gave them power and authority .... and sent them out to preach the kingdom and to heal, and they departed and went out through the villages preaching the gospel and healing everywhere."

"Afterwards the Lord appointed seventy-two others and sent them on ahead, two by two, into every town and place where He Himself was about to come"

.... "The seventy-two returned with joy saying 'Lord even the demons were subject to us in your name' " (Luke 10v1&17).

As Jesus began to warn His disciples of His coming suffering, death and return to His Father, He also assured them of another helper and counsellor, another of the same kind, namely the Holy Spirit especially in chapters 14 to 16 of John. He, the Holy Spirit, would teach them all things, lead them into all truth and enable them to do His works. There were many other occasions during Christ's Ministry when the

Holy Spirit had been manifested: e.g. His baptism . In the synagogue at Nazareth He had read from the prophet Isaiah: "The Spirit of the Lord is upon me because He has anointed me to preach the good news to the poor" and Jesus concludes "Today the Scripture has been fulfilled in your hearing." (Luke. 4v18) On another occasion He is talking about human fathers knowing how to give good gifts to their children and concludes: "How much more will the Heavenly Father give the Holy Spirit to those that ask Him!" (Luke 1v13).

Before His ascension Jesus in Matthew 28v18-20 says: "All authority in Heaven and earth has been given to me .... go and make disciples of all nations teaching them to obey everything I have commanded you (to preach the Kingdom and heal the sick). And lo, I am with you always (through the Holy Spirit)." Jesus assures them of the necessary help and empowering: "I am going to send you what my father has promised .... Stay in the city until you are clothed with power from on high" (Luke. 24v49). Jesus confirms this in the first chapter of Acts: "before many days you shall be baptised with the Holy Spirit" and three verses later "you shall receive power when the Holy Spirit has come upon you" (Acts. 1v5.8).

So the disciples obeyed (obedience is always important) and were continually in the temple praising God. "When the day of Pentecost was come, they were all together in one place. And suddenly a sound came from Heaven like the rush of a mighty wind, for it filled the house where they were sitting. And there appeared to them tongues as of fire, distributed and resting on each one of them. And they were all filled with the Holy Spirit and began to speak in other tongues, as the Spirit gave them utterance" (Acts. 2v1,4). This Pentecost experience almost defies description, and still does today when people experience it. Some of these strange events would have had greater significance for those Jews than they have for us Gentiles. The wind is another word for spirit bringing new life as in the valley of dry bones in Ezekiel 37. Fire symbolises purification and power. The gift of tongues enabled the people from the different parts of the Roman Empire to hear the message in their own language; a reversal of the experience at the Tower of Babel which scattered and confused all the people in disunity.

One of the gifts of the Spirit described in Romans 12, 1 Cor. 12, Eph. 4 and 1 Peter 4, is the gift of preaching. Peter had often been the spokesman for the disciples, usually in short impulsive statements, sometimes inspired, more often not. Now that he has been filled with the Holy Spirit at Pentecost Peter immediately lifts up his voice and speaks to all the people who were gathered to see what the commotion was. Peter preaches an inspired sermon which goes right to the hearts of the hearers to such an extent that three thousand repent, are baptised and filled with Spirit and added to their numbers.

Another gift of the Holy Spirit is that of healing and in the next chapter in the Acts of the Apostles we have the thrilling story of the beggar lame from birth who receives healing through Peter and John in the name of Jesus Christ of Nazareth and accompanies them into the Temple "leaping and praising God." So at the very beginning of the Church's life we find them fulfilling Christ's specific command to preach the good news of the Kingdom and heal the sick. As the Gospel of St Mark says as it ends: "they went forth and preached everywhere, while the Lord worked with them, and confirmed the message by the signs that attended it."

The Holy Spirit of God did not suddenly appear on the scene for the first time at Pentecost. He is God and so was at the beginning with God in the same way that Jesus was. He appears at the beginning of the creation story. "The Spirit of God was moving over the face of the waters" (Gen. 1v2). He is frequently referred to throughout the Old Testament playing His part in working out God's purpose through a particular person, at a particular time for a particular task. but at Pentecost, as Joel had prophesied God poured out His Spirit on ALL flesh. Thanks to what Jesus had done for us in taking our sins on Himself the Holy Spirit of God would fill any Christian who would ask and receive. And so with this empowering and equipping of the Holy Spirit the early church expanded rapidly as it preached the good news of the Kingdom and healed the sick. Unfortunately as the centuries rolled on, in some parts of the church some form of ritual, some aspect of organisation or administration, some point of doctrine becomes more important than receiving God's Holy Spirit or even a substitute for Him. Those parts of the Church soon lose power and direction. Fortunately in recent years much of the church has rediscovered the all-importance of the Holy Spirit in equal status with the Father and Jesus. In very recent years the popular Alpha Course from Holy Trinity Brompton has greatly helped in this. Often churches use the facilities of the Harnhill Centre for the Holy Spirit Away Day on the Alpha Course. For one person from a Wiltshire church it transformed her life. Let Julie tell the story for herself:

"If I could have got out of going to Harnhill, I would have. I approached George with at least two excuses not to go, but thankfully he did not allow me that option. I began to look forward to the day for little more than a break from the children. "

"Since May I had been enjoying our new routine of regularly attending church. However, I felt no real direction. I had been enjoying the Alpha Course – though I was doing it for want of a good enough reason to say no. Often we heard talk of people "changing," and yes, actually it sounded wonderful. In fact the friends we had made at church did seem to me wonderful, with sincerity and depth of emotion I aspired to or liked to think I shared. But the reality of being like that, or experiencing a "change" was, or seemed to me at least, unlikely. Or certainly not around the corner .... Or even up the road at Harnhill."

"I wouldn't have called myself self-satisfied before, but certainly level headed, trustworthy, generous and even happy, and nearly all the time.

Some aspects of my life were problematical, but those were the bits that were not on show, and didn't matter so much anyway, surely everyone has days when they cannot cope or can't be bothered."

"The day at Harnhill was much as I had expected it to be, worship, prayers, talks, lunch. None of this has ever come alive to me before, it has only ever been faultless, but quite flat, theory. It was to my surprise and total relief that I started crying quietly as we were singing in the realisation of how much I was hurting inside. That my external calm demeanour had become a disguise for inner turmoil. Suddenly and from somewhere I found the courage to admit to myself that I had had enough, I was not living a whole life."

"All the aspects of my life that had been weighing me down, that I was accepting as part of life, I realised could be handed over. I could see clearly, and it came all at once (as I had sceptically thought until this point, was too simplistic a thing to happen to anybody) that I could step forward from this place and be free."

"We were invited forward for ministry, until then a totally alien concept for me, to be avoided if possible. I went forward eagerly, crying and crying until peace descended and my load was shed. "

"I walked straight outside into the sharp, dusky, Gloucestershire air and reciprocated a long stare with a sheep. I knew something profound had just taken place in my life. I had taken off a boiler suit of cares and been left with .... myself."

"The next morning, having lain peacefully awake in the early hours, I emerged into the day feeling anxious that I would somehow lose this new perspective and return to the me of two days before. I spent much of the morning walking around tentatively, slightly self-conscious, and all the while this incredible new feeling bursting from me. The Vicar asked me at the end of the Remembrance Day service that next day if I was "still glowing" – and there I was sure that everyone could see me flashing bright like a beacon."

"Seven days have passed (as I write this) and to me they have been incredible days. Days of patience and love. I am still grinning and no longer entertain the possibility of going back."

"I never thought, expected or even wanted this to happen to me. And now I cannot believe how fortunate I am that it has."

"I have been given possession of my life."

Many similar stories can be recalled, though they are always slightly different. Each individual is unique and God deals with each person according to his or her particular need.

Sue from another local church was also reluctant to go to their Holy Spirit Day in their Alpha Course. She had plenty of other things to do on her Saturdays after working all week. However she went and as with Julie she went up for prayer at the end which she had never done before. However with Sue nothing seemed to happen at the time. It was only when she got home and prayed "properly" for the first time about her problems and then praised God for His answers that the Holy Spirit began to work in her life: "That night I slept as I have never slept before." Next day in church she could not take her thoughts off Jesus and that afternoon taking her dogs for a walk into the countryside, she felt so close to the God of creation and realised her life had been transformed. The Holy Spirit's work with Sue and Julie is not finished yet, or with any of us. His creative work in us continues. The gifts of the Spirit are to be sought. These gifts are not actually possessed like talents or abilities, though God can and does greatly use and enhance such talents. But the gifts of the Spirit are supernaturally given by God as the situation requires. Peter was given three in quick succession: tongues, preaching and healing. Likewise any spirit-filled Christian when faced by a situation requiring a gift of the spirit can be given it instantaneously. As a curate without knowing anything about the ministry of Christian healing I was confronted by a boy of twelve, desperately ill, with only six weeks to live. I felt compelled to pray for his healing and he was healed. That was not through any ability of mine. I felt quite helpless; it was the work of the Holy Spirit. It was God's choice and God's doing. So with many Christians confronted by a situation that requires it, they can be given the gift of healing in an instant. The young Asian woman who was used by God to pray for Jennifer Rees Larcombe, did not want to do it, had never done it before and did it in the wrong way according to the books on Christian healing, yet Jennifer got out of her wheel chair after eight years, folded it up and carried it out to the car. It was not that young woman's gift, it was not her doing, but God's through His Holy Spirit. It was His gift, His doing through that young woman.

Much the same goes for other supernatural gifts. I don't reckon to have a prophetic ministry, but I have found myself in situations which seemed to require a prophecy and He has given me the first two or three words and prompted me to speak them out and then others have followed. Similarly with the interpretation of tongues, words of knowledge and wisdom. The gift has been given at the time God required it for a particular situation. The gift of tongues differs in that it is mainly for personal use and seems to be a permanent possession. Such gifts of the Spirit are obviously important to equip the church and are to be eagerly sought by those who have been filled with God's Holy Spirit.

The fruit of the Spirit is equally important but different. The fruit is not instantaneous, but like the fruit in an orchard takes time to grow and mature. And we note the word "fruit" is singular not plural. It is one package. You cannot have peace and no patience. It's like an orange with nine segments, each of a different flavour; love, joy, peace, patience, kindness, goodness, faithfulness, gentleness and self-control (Gal. 5v22). All these Christ-like qualities go together to make a mature

Christian. The growth of Christ's character within us is the work of the Holy Spirit so that over the years the Holy Spirit transforms us into His (Christ's) likeness (2 Cor. 3v18). The image of God is restored in us.

The work of the Holy Spirit of God in the life of an individual, or in the life of a church, or in a secular situation, is a marvel to behold. It is a demonstration of the restoring power of God through Jesus Christ. The word power so often used in connection with the Holy Spirit in the New Testament is "dunamis" in the Greek, from which we get our word "dynamite." The dynamite of the Holy Spirit breaks open the hard shell of closed lives and situations, shatters the bondages that binds and enables the restorative work of Jesus Christ to take effect and bring together man and woman and God.

Coffee Break on a Holy Spirit Day

God and Man

We now consider the broken relationships between God and men and women. This separation began when Adam and Eve disobeyed God in the garden of Eden. As a result of their disobedience in eating the forbidden fruit in the garden they experienced guilt and shame: "the man and his wife hid themselves from the presence of the Lord God" (Gen. 3v8). They chose to separate themselves from God. That is what sin does, it separates us from God. But God sought them out and continues to seek us out. And there is only one way that broken relationships can be redeemed and restored, and that is through the mediation initiated by God and involving the very costly sacrifice of his Son Jesus as stated in chapter 2.

The sense of separation from God is still felt by men and women. Augustine of Hippo in the 5th century expressed it in his well-known words: "Our hearts are restless until they find their rest in you." Others talk of a great emptiness inside themselves, a God-shaped hole that only He can fill. Many have a sense of guilt. Some speak of a great gulf between them and God across which a bridge is needed. That bridge is Jesus Christ. The Living Bible translates 1 Tim 2v5 in these words: "God is on one side and all the people on the other, and Christ Jesus, himself man, is in between to bring them together." A hundred years ago Professor Moberly of Oxford, in his great book "Atonement and Personality," echoes Saint Paul when he speaks of "Christ being made sin .... to restore men to God," he later adds: "He is never not incarnate .... His role of mediator is permanent." He took the consequences and penalty of peoples' sins upon Himself on the cross and crucified them and rose victorious over them once and for all. His restoration of the broken relationship between people and God is always available to those who come to him in penitence and faith. Faith in the New Testament according to C.H. Dodd in his commentary on Romans means trust like that of a little child toward its parents.

Jesus has done all that is necessary to restore us to God but there has to be a response on our part. He says: "Come to me all who labour and are heavy laden," and He adds "take my yoke upon you, and learn from me; for I am gentle and lowly in heart, and you will find rest for your souls. For my yoke is easy and my burden is light" (Mat. 11v28-30). That can equally correctly be translated "my yoke is well-fitting" and there is a lovely old legend which says that over the carpenter's shop in Nazareth was a sign reading: "Well-fitting yokes made here." Farmers for miles around, it is said, would come to Jesus to have him make yokes for their oxen for they knew they would fit perfectly and in consequence they would get better work out of their oxen. Whether there is any truth in the legend or not Jesus has for each one of us a yoke which fits perfectly. He has the perfect plan for each one of us which, with the help of the Holy Spirit, will enable each of us to fulfil God's purpose for us which will be totally satisfying.

The way of receiving that yoke from Jesus is to come to Him to confess all our sins and to receive from Him His wonderful free forgiveness and to totally surrender our whole lives to Him. There is always a danger of our holding some part of our life back in which case we will not receive our full blessing; the yoke will not fit perfectly. Another way of thinking of this surrendering our lives to Jesus is from Rev. 3v20, where Jesus stands at the door of our hearts and knocks. Holman Hunt in his famous picture "Christ the Light of the World" depicts this scene and shows there is no handle on the outside of the door. It has to be opened by us from the inside. Some who open the door to Jesus are quite happy to allow Him into the front room, but not keen for Him to go into the kitchen or the cupboard under the stairs or other dirty or dusty corners. Only as we give Him total possession of our lives do we receive his full gift of abundant new life.

The ability of Jesus Christ to restore us from our fallen state has been described in another way in a rather amusing piece of anonymous writing I came across some years ago entitled "The Pit," it goes something like this:

"A man fell into a pit and could not get himself out.

A subjective person came along and said 'I feel for you down there.'

An objective person came along and said 'It's logical that someone would fall down there.'

A Pharisee said 'Only bad people fall into pits.'

A news reporter wanted an exclusive story on his pit.

Confucius said: 'If you had listened to me, you would not be in that pit.'

Buddha said: 'Your pit is only a state of mind.'

A realist said: 'That is a pit.'

A scientist calculated the forces necessary to get him out of the pit.

A geologist told him to appreciate the rock strata in the pit.

A tax man asked if he was paying taxes on the pit.

The council inspector asked if he had a permit to dig a pit.

An evasive person came along and avoided the subject of the pit altogether.

A self-pitying person said: 'You haven't seen anything until you have seen my pit.'

An optimist said: 'Things could be worse.'

A pessimist said: 'Things will get worse.'

Jesus, seeing the man, got down into the pit with him and helped him out but died in the process."

Only Jesus can help us get out of our pit, no one else. So many people seek to find an answer in all sorts of other ways and other people. Some of them find their way to Harnhill. They may come seeking help with some problem or sickness. There they find Jesus and so the help they need, for only Jesus can help them through the Holy Spirit. Evangelism, proclaiming the good news of Jesus, and healing, are two sides of the same coin. Both are aspects of salvation.

Anna was one who eventually found Jesus and the help she needed at Harnhill as she tells:

"When I was younger I was very anti anything to do with God. I didn't believe and had no time for any kind of religious stuff. I thought people who had anything to do with religion were caught up in a pretend world of their own, were kidding themselves and couldn't face up to reality! The thought of me believing in God was non-existent and would have horrified me."

"I have had lots of problems with eating disorders, self-harm and depression. I had medical help, which was a great support. It helped me to understand my eating disorder, face up to the fact that I had one and helped me realise I was not the only person who had one. And it also helped physically. Unfortunately I became very good at lying because I didn't want and wasn't ready, to get better."

"All I thought about, cared about and dreamt about was food. In one sense I liked being trapped in a world of food; it was safe, secure and had reachable goals. In another sense I hated food, didn't need it, thought that it was the only problem and thought that if it didn't exist everything would be perfect and I would be happy. I felt very guilty as I knew that I was a complete nightmare to live with."

"My concentration and commitment were rubbish, I was constantly swapping courses. I didn't want to be alive but seeing as I was, I thought I might as well try and be useful and always tried to please others. I wanted to escape from being me and thought that by making new starts I would turn into a new person."

"Out of the blue and interest I wrote a letter to an island asking for any kind of job. Not long later a lady phoned up and basically said start at the weekend. She didn't even ask for references. Mum told me that she said a prayer when she posted the letter and it did cross my mind: was it the prayer or was it fluke? I desperately needed to escape, I knew there was no way I could stay where I was or like I was any longer. The islands were really beautiful. I was slowly becoming less obsessed with food and had a lot of time to think about things like where the world comes from, what's the point in life, why do we live? We just get born and then die. I also realised that food wasn't the problem but that I was trapped in myself and couldn't escape from being me. As I was becoming less obsessed with food and trying not to use it I was turning more to self-harm."

"Back home I started my A-levels again and decided if I had friends then everything would be fine. I got friends and this didn't happen. Physically I was fine now although food and self-harm were still lingering. It was weird because superficially I was a lot happier due to being on a high dose of anti-depressants but underneath I still hated life, didn't see the point or a reason for anything. I changed courses yet again."

"My Mum had recently found her faith and in the Summer she went on a parish weekend to Harnhill Christian Healing Centre. I was thinking about quitting the nursing course I had not long started, was feeling really trapped in myself, despondent and depressed. Mum said that she really thought that Harnhill might be able to help me. I knew I had nothing to lose and was up for anything that might be able to help. I had become more open-minded about different people's beliefs as after all, the world had to come from somewhere. Although I didn't believe in God I had started to talk to others and ask what did make the world. I refused to call Him God as there was no way I was going to be associated with being religious or have anything to do with religion. I went to Harnhill for two weekends and both times sorted out lots of stuff and came back much more relaxed and at ease. I also came back with a faith, believing in God. I realised that I belonged to God and that He had a plan for me. For the first time in years I felt different inside. It took me about a month to work out that this different feeling was excitement. Just seeing how people had given their lives to God, like at Harnhill showed me that He is there and that it is nothing to do with being religious but that it is a personal relationship with Jesus and through Him, with God. I had also started reading autobiographies and was seeing the difference and the miracles God had performed in lives."

"If it hadn't been for God I would definitely have quit my nursing course. I failed an exam, which I retook and again did badly. I begged God that I would fail again so I would have a truthful excuse to leave this course! While retaking the exam I had the next modules assignments and did a deal with God that if I failed one (I knew I had failed the exam) then I would quit, if I passed all I'd accept the fact that He wanted me to stay on the same course. I did pass, getting 40% in the exam which is the pass mark."

"I moved out of home and was meeting lots of new people. I just really couldn't understand why God was being so nice to me. I was making friends who just accepted me for being me even though I hardly ever spoke. I started to find things more difficult again as I was trying hard not to abuse myself and was asking God to punish me instead. But He didn't. I wanted to escape from God but couldn't. I thought He was great for others but had made a mistake with me. I kept trying to pull myself together which got nowhere. I was still trapped. Mum suggested that I went back to Harnhill. I went for a week even though I was convinced God had given up on me and didn't want me there. I felt very guilty but didn't know what else to do."

"At the end of the Tuesday at Harnhill I was getting panicky as I realised that there was no way I could get rid of all the heavy hurt that was inside. I got given a couple of Bible verses that spoke to me. I got down on my knees and really prayed to God to help me and show me what He wanted me to do. I would do anything He wanted but I couldn't carry on living and feeling like this, I felt despondent and hated life."

"The next day we had a talk through which God spoke to me loads, I also had dreams and realised that there was a lot I didn't want to face up to but needed to sort out. Before this the Bible seemed dull, irrelevant, full of long words and complicated language but it just came to life, was really exciting and there were loads of messages in it from Jesus to me! In the counselling session on Thursday we prayed through lots of things. I realised that Jesus loves me all the time (whatever I or anybody else thought!), that He had a purpose in life for me, that He would always be with me and that He wanted to be my friend. Everything is up to Him not me. We also prayed that afternoon that Jesus would make it obvious to me that He was with me during the rest of the day. I decided to go on a long walk. It was amazing! Inside I felt like a completely different person. I noticed that in every direction the sky was grey and dull except for where I was. Directly above me there was a small bright, blue gap in the clouds with the sun shining through to the spot where I was. It continued to be like this for the whole way. I must have walked for three to four hours and the wind was constantly blowing in the opposite direction. I also saw loads of deer and had a very special afternoon knowing that this was Jesus and that He was with me. It was completely amazing I had never felt nor imagined I would ever feel that happy. It was great I just felt so light and free."

"Since then through Jesus I am getting to know God. He is constantly working in my life and changing me. All I have to do is what I am told. Even when I do get down I know that if I keep my eyes fixed on Jesus He will help me through and I look at this world as a steppingstone to greater things. My old attitude to life and people has completely switched round and relationships with others are constantly getting better. I still can't believe how much my life has changed round and done a full circle. I never thought I would even get out of the bottom of the black holes I was in but thanks to God (and everyone at Harnhill!) I now have a future and a life and I am free."

Jesus said "I am the Way, the Truth and the Life." He also said "The truth will make you free." Anna has discovered that, as have countless others at Harnhill and elsewhere.

It is so exciting to see Jesus rescue people and sort out their problems. Yet in another way it is also natural. It is what is meant to happen. It is why God's only Son Jesus came to earth and lived among us and died and rose and ascended. We too have to go through a process of dying to the old life and rising again in a new life in Jesus. And often the very difficulties and sicknesses can help us in that process enabling us to acknowledge our inability to help ourselves out of our mess and turn to the only person who can completely help us: Jesus. We see this process go on day after day at Harnhill.

Recently our sitting room, a few hundred yards from Harnhill Manor, has become an extension of the Centre now that my wife has become more lame. We carry on with our gentle prayer counselling here.

One day a vivacious blonde, a very talented fifty-year-old, sat on our sofa. She had come from Sweden at the age of seventeen and been a top model. After five years she married a very rich man and had two children by him but after a while had agreed to part company. Sometime later she had married another rich man and had another two children. They quickly got through their money, partly through drink and then he went off with a local waitress. She was left high and dry. Lena said: "I have been a millionaire twice, I have lived in a castle and experienced every luxury. Now I have nothing; and yet I have everything, because I have Jesus."

Two days later sitting on the same sofa was a man of about forty. He had been on drugs for much of his life, had indulged in sexual perversion, experienced great guilt and deep depression. Yet the Lord had never let him go. At his request I had visited him regularly in the psychiatric ward of a hospital a year or so before and now here he sat on our sofa in his right mind. He suddenly said: "I am so happy, I have never been so happy and yet I am not on dope. I never knew you could be so happy without dope." He had discovered that Jesus was far more satisfying and could make him far happier than drugs ever could and without the complications.

Week by week people pour into Harnhill to the healing services, the training days, the prayer counselling, the conferences or they come to stay a few days. Day after day Jesus continues His reconciling, restoring work, bringing people back into a loving relationship with His Heavenly Father through the Holy Spirit.

Claire likened her few days at Harnhill to that of going to hospital:

"In many respects my visit to Harnhill was like spending time in hospital. The gentle structure of the timetable and the caring but professional approach of the counselling team promoted the Centre's purpose – to enable you to experience the power of Jesus Christ."

"I arrived at Harnhill weighed down by the burden of sin and bearing old festering wounds, some that had hindered me since childhood. The Lord Jesus met me when I arrived. He wrapped me in His love and nursed me through the process of reopening those wounds. Painful though it was I was constantly reassured by His presence and of His love for me."

"In time for the first counselling session I was ready to receive His healing touch. When we are physically sick we are prepared to do what it takes to be well again, even if it means going through the indignity and vulnerability of being on the operating table. This is how I felt. I was desperately aware of my great need to be healed and was now prepared to cast away my pride and come, naked and vulnerable before the Lord."

"During the final session I could feel His presence as I confessed my sins to Him and then allowed Him to minister to my wounds. My counsellors were the Lord's handmaidens and like good theatre nurses ministered to me only through His instruction and under His loving authority. I was forgiven and healed."

"Leaving Harnhill was difficult. Even though I had been healed I still felt fragile and sore, just as after any surgery. It was also difficult to readjust to the faster pace of the world outside. I have since found that

The Warden, the Rev'd Paul Springate, speaking in the Barn

it takes time to learn how to live without the old wounds and to break old behaviour patterns. The struggle is constant and ongoing. It will of course always be necessary to come to the Lord for forgiveness and healing. After my visit to Harnhill, however, I am certain that the victory has been won. I know that Jesus died for me; to wash away my sins and to heal my wounds. Yes. He really does love me that much."

God the Father loves to be in fellowship with us. For that purpose we were created. Jesus has made it possible. The Holy Spirit enables us to lay hold of that possibility.

Man and Man

Broken relationships between people and between nations fill the headlines of our newspapers every day. They provide some of the worst problems for those in leadership as they seek to improve conditions in communities, in this country and in the world. Conflict is present also in families with children running away from home and the divorce rate at an all time high.

It was a domestic conflict which started off this chain of broken relationships when Adam blamed Eve for their disobedience of God: "The woman you gave to be with me, she gave me the fruit of the tree and I ate" Adam tells God in Gen. 3v12. Men have been putting the blame on their wives ever since, and I must plead guilty to this at times. In the next chapter of Genesis domestic conflict reaches a new level as Cain slays his brother Abel in anger and jealously. Disobeying God was beginning to lead to the consequence God had warned Adam and Eve that it would have: death. Thanks to Jesus it does not have to stay that way. He died for us. He took the consequences of all mankind: anger and jealously and sin on himself on the cross and rose victorious over them. As we turn to Him in genuine repentance we receive complete forgiveness, a new start, and a new life. Many people come to Harnhill with deep domestic relationship problems. A young couple, Nick and Debbie who had a little boy just starting school, were one such couple. Nick writes:

"Debbie had previous experience of Christian counselling which she felt had helped her. I thought it actually made things worse. At this point we went back to Debbie's support group at our church who suggested we came to Harnhill.

Our life at home was dominated by arguments and frequent violent fights. Debbie first went to Harnhill as a resident for a Healing Week and I was impressed by how much better our relationship was afterwards."

"Debbie then arranged to receive regular prayer counselling and the first meeting was set up for a Saturday morning. On the way there our car had a problem with its thermostat and we arrived late. I dropped Debbie off and went to get the car fixed in Cirencester. When I went back to collect her, she explained that Arthur and Letty had been expecting me to be there also, which surprised me, because I felt that the problems in our relationship were all as a result of her background, and so why did I need counselling?"

"I had a very real fear of talking to people and generally don't open up to people about close personal issues. I really didn't want to go; our Vicar Colin Blake, came with us to the first meeting, as support for me."

"The prayer counselling we received was very gentle, and as we talked, Arthur and Letty kept gently reminding us that we should bring the Lord into all areas of our lives. We left that first session tired, and encouraged. Of course things didn't change overnight, and, as we came back from subsequent sessions, we became very close to Arthur and Letty and valued their advice and balanced perspective."

"The Lord moved very powerfully through these two quiet people, and almost un-noticed our lives changed as Debbie and I grew closer together as a couple and in the Lord. The violence stopped and we learned to respect each other and care for each other."

"Debbie had the wisdom to encourage me to go to Harnhill as a resident, and I attended a Healing Weekend in August of 1998. I was refreshed and touched by the teaching as never before."

"We owe our marriage to the people at Harnhill and the gentle peace of God they helped bring into our lives."

A little later a rather older couple came who had been deeply divided for a long time. In the first session they almost immediately started quarrelling violently. We had to separate them and then see them separately for a session or two and then together again. There were several very difficult and stormy sessions but also a little progress.

Once they had accepted that their only hope was to turn to Jesus, immediately a few issues began to surface in the mind as their tempers began to rise and allow the Holy Spirit to have control. Whatever the issues neither has the complete answer, only Jesus. Once they had accepted this I said: "You must now work it out for yourselves with Jesus. It is no good coming for more sessions with us and just going over the same ground." In the middle of that last session the woman stormed out. After a while I went out, but it was some time before I found her. After a few choice words she agreed to come back and the session was finished amicably with prayer. We did not arrange another session, though they could get back to us and arrange another meeting if they really needed it. They did not come back but we did receive two lovely letters telling us how their relationship was wonderfully better.

Extra-marital affairs are all too common and often accepted by today's society as normal. But that is not God's view as clearly stated in the Bible. Just to denounce such relationships from the pulpit does not often have the desired results. Sue, when she came to Harnhill was accepted, loved, and then decided herself it was right to give up her affair with a man and so be fully restored to the Lord and His purpose for her as she tells: "At a time when I had left an unhappy marriage and, although a christian, was involved in an affair that I knew was wrong, a number of people asked me the same question: "Have you been to Harnhill yet?" At that time I had no idea what Harnhill was but when the last person to ask me added that she was "going next Friday" and did I want to come? I thought I had better see for myself what this place was. I attended the Healing Service and was surprised at the part where the minister gave out words of knowledge that had been given to those praying together before the service: I had never heard that sort of thing before. I was even more surprised when one of those words was that there had been a picture given of a bluebell wood, the minister said that God must have His eye on someone who lived in a bluebell wood. At that time I lived in a remote cottage in a nature reserve which was a bluebell wood! My friend nudged me and said: "That's you!" I nodded and felt a mixture of embarrassment and excitement. I did not accept the invitation to go to the front for prayer, it all seemed too difficult to face but I knew clearly that the Lord had brought me there to sort out my life."

"I started to attend Friday morning healing services fairly regularly and, eventually, dared to go up for prayer. I don't remember who prayed with me that first time but, what I do remember clearly is their acceptance of me as I was; there was no sense of shock or judgement at my situation, there was simply an overwhelming love as they held me to the Lord. It was not long before I realised that I wanted to have prayer counselling at Harnhill, even though I was not entirely sure what that involved! Again I met with the same acceptance and love. I was not judged, I was listened to and prayed with by my two counsellors as I started my journey back into the Lord's way. The prayer counselling brought everything into focus for me, each session was an exhausting experience in which they helped me to face my past failures and the challenge of obedience to the Lord."

"Through the prayer counselling and the teaching and quiet days I attended at Harnhill I was able to see that the Lord is of supreme importance and He gave me the strength to end the affair I was in and be restored to Himself. Since that time I have continued to be encouraged and instructed by the teaching and prayer at Harnhill; now much of what I learned there I pass on to others when I teach in my own fellowship."

"For me, and I have no doubt, for countless others, Harnhill provided the vital ministry of restoring my faith and discipleship at a time when I had lost my way. One direct result of this was that I was able to hear the Lord's call to China about three years later. In fact, He had first called me to China some thirty-five years earlier when I was 14; and, although I had married and brought up a family, that first call and my love for China had never left me – it had just been buried deep down somewhere. The ministry I received at Harnhill not only restored my walk with the Lord but, by showing me the love of Jesus in a fresh way, it gave me a hunger to know Him better and while continuing to be built up by the ministry and teaching at Harnhill I also went to other places where there was good teaching and, at one of these, a conference run by Ellel Ministries, I heard again the call to go to China. For Christians called to work for the Lord in China today one route in is teaching English in a University there; I trained to teach English and was sent to a University in a city in N.W China. As an English teacher my room was constantly full of students wanting conversation practice and there were many opportunities to share my faith in answer to their questions. I have now completed my time in China and returned home."

"I believe that Our Lord is always wanting to lead us on in His service and fullness of life but that through our own disobedience and lack of trust we may often step out of His way and fail to know that fullness. That was my position when I first came to Harnhill and it was through the ministry that I received there that I was enabled to find His way for my life; I am so grateful to the dear friend who took me to that Friday morning service and to those committed, loving counsellors who ministered to me in His Name."

Sue is now in leadership in her Methodist church in this country.

Others who serve at Harnhill like Sue have felt called to serve overseas for a while. Elizabeth has had three or four short spells in Uganda.

Others have been in China, Burma, Thailand, Eastern Europe, especially the Ukraine. One couple hit the headlines by being captured in a tribal kidnapping in the Yemen. They said: "We were their guests and that is how they treated us except we were locked in." When released, after a brief spell at home, they went back there. They are now home again and help at Harnhill as part of the non-resident voluntary helpers.

Some human relationships have been ravished far more severely, but even they can be healed by Jesus. I think of some who have come to Harnhill as rape victims. Then there was the mother who came to a Wednesday evening healing service carrying her 8-year old daughter in her arms as though she was a baby. The girl had been severely traumatised and terrified through occult practice at a Hallowe'en party the evening before. The mother had come a long way to Harnhill not knowing where else to go. To another Wednesday service came a woman in anguish, again from some distance; her daughter had been murdered a day or two beforehand. A person who had suffered many various traumas but has received healing from Jesus is Jeremy in his late forties:

"My father was a successful jeweller. My main early memory of him is of leaving home either to work or in the evening to go to one of his many functions dressed up in his finery. At the age of eleven I was sent to boarding school in my own town, an odd experience as I could see my parent's home from my dormitory window. I missed my twin sister and my mother, who unbeknown to me, was very much against me going to this school where my father had been, and now was a governor. The school was run by Catholic brothers. My experience there was a mixture of fear and boredom. There was punishment and punishing. With the environment of Catholicism the church was used as punishment, for God was a punishing God. There was nothing loving there. The brothers used both strap and cane to enforce their power. This transferred itself to the boys who ran their own kind of regime. I was hung by a rope within a few weeks of being there. I learnt to defend myself either by power or deceit, becoming an accomplished liar, always dodging reality. Worse than this I was sexually abused by one of the brothers and this had an effect on the rest of my life, a secret that I kept for the next twenty-five years."

"Every aspect of my life was affected. Problems arose in relationships, work, self-esteem and the constant need to get approval from other people, especially my father. At the age of 41, after another failed relationship (four engagements over twenty years) and my mother dying, I took an overdose to try and take my life. After the best part of a year under psychiatric care both in and out of hospital, little or no progress had been made."

"Then I met Nick, a pastor. I approached him to give some money to whoever was the poorest member of his congregation for Christmas, and he simply asked: "Why?" Five hours and many tears later and with the address of Harnhill, I left with the feeling there was some hope."

"The tarot card readers, the astrologers, the spiritualist healers had all failed me as had the more conventional counsellors. Now I phoned Harnhill to book in for a week. I spoke to John and it was obvious that it would be some time before I could get a booking. Well, it wasn't going to happen, but I left my address and phone number and thought I would forget all about it. God had other ideas. The following day John phoned and said they had a cancellation for the next week – perfect, I had no time to think."

"I went very reluctantly on the Monday afternoon. The first person I met was Rob and immediately felt a warm unconditional love from this man. But all the old fears of a punishing God reared their heads. I saw all these smiling faces and these Bibles and wondered what I had let myself in for. I thankfully remembered I had put my golf clubs in the back of my car as a means of escape. The prayer counselling was different from anything I had experienced before. There were two people and a third was being prayed to, namely Jesus. I was told I was unique and precious and so the process began. But I was cynical towards anything that was different. I was beginning to think seriously about my golf clubs. Then on Wednesday evening a healing service was announced: "A what?" I thought, but I went along wondering what might happen. The singing was cheerful and good, so that was alright. Then John talked of words of knowledge and prophesies. One hit me both in its humour and its accuracy. John said; "There is someone here who wants to give their life to God to the extent of giving up their golf clubs." Who knew? Who had looked? I went forward for prayer and God started His work in me. We had quite a party and the weight of guilt, unforgiveness and hopelessness left me as Jesus held me in his arms."

"Now, some five years later I am on the ministry team that is part of Holy Trinity Brompton and visit prisons. My life has completely changed. The struggle goes on but that other person in the counselling room is always part of my life: Jesus."

In Jeremy's story, and in Sue's and others, we see that Our Heavenly Father loves to heal us through His Holy Spirit when we turn wholeheartedly to His Son Jesus. He delights to heal us for our own benefit. But the process of opening up to Him means that His purpose for us can then be fulfilled which nearly always means that others benefit also. This is in Jo's case as well:

"My parents had married in a fortnight during the second world war. They soon discovered it was a mistake, and were going to give their first born son, my brother, up for adoption and divorce when I happened. After the war they emigrated to Canada, leaving me and my brother in England for about a year. Those two events set the tone of our relationship, and my childhood was one of physical, sexual and emotional abuse. I grew up in a very non-Christian household, but was

Jo in the Garden at Harnhill

sent to school as it was the only form of private education at that time in Canada. My parents had both been educated privately, hence the choice. I used to go into church at the age of 6 and 7 and just absorb the peace and quiet on my way home from school."

"I grew up with three more brothers arriving after me and looked after them a lot of the time. I left home as soon as I could and got my own rented flat. Life was reasonable. I met and married Pete in a ten month period, then settled down. We moved back to England four years after we married, and three years later started a family. It was the best time of my life! I had struggled about having children, had a nervous breakdown because I was denying myself the chance as I felt I would abuse them as I had been abused. After some psychiatric help I felt safe to embark on children. We had two girls with a fifteen-month gap and I loved them so much. I never felt like hitting them, and started to get angry about what had been done to me. Kate, our second daughter, developed cancer at the age of 11, and after a two-year battle, died. My life ended I felt. God spoke to me through Kate in a dream, and I became a Christian a year after she died. Soon after that, I saw there was a weeding and worship day at Harnhill. I love gardening so came along. During the course of the day, the head gardener mentioned the need of more help. I felt this was heaven on earth, and offered. Unfortunately (I thought at the time) the only day I had free, which was the Friday, and half the day was taken up with the Healing Service!

I wanted to garden, not go to church! Still, I went the first Friday, reluctantly and my life was changed for ever. There was a word given which I tried to ignore, but the floodgates just opened. I sat paralysed in my seat unable to move for the pain. I felt a gentle hand on my shoulder, and went up for prayer. I could hardly speak for the pain. After some prayer, it was suggested that perhaps I could come in-house for a week's prayer ministry. There was a space immediately. I took time off work and my life was given back to me by God in that place slowly, gently and oh so lovingly. The most healing aspect was the love – God's love – mirrored in the eyes of my prayer ministers. They held me in my unbearable pain – the first time in my life anyone ever had. Over a two or three year period I continued to come in house, and to see outside prayer counsellors, and in that time felt the Lord was giving me back the years the locusts had stolen."

"The second healing aspect was the forgiveness I worked through towards my parents, in particular, and the world in general. With God's Grace and a lot of prayer support, I was able to forgive and therefore love my parents. I saw that what they had done to me was as a result of their pain and unhappiness, and not because I was awful and unlovable. The inner peace and joy that knowledge gave me are indescribable – all in God's loving circle."

"I now am on the ministry team, and do some outside prayer counselling – slowly, gently increasing at the Lord's pace. I work with the guests on a Tuesday night, and have a deep involvement with my home church. Harnhill have become the family I never really had. I feel I am surrounded by love and acceptance and this is so healing on an on-going level. I am not saying it is living happily ever after. There are times when I am so angry with God. He just gently shows me the times he carried me – the peace of that church as a frightened six-year old child needing a sanctuary, the love of the nuns at school, marriage to a very caring man who has stayed by me during all the tempestuous years of being angry and not knowing why. And most importantly giving me a caring, loving place like Harnhill. Every time someone hugs me or returns my smile, I grow inside. I feel affirmed and loved where I am, not where they think I should be. I owe my life to Harnhill's love, which is Christ's love."

Jo's reference above to "the times He carried me" echoes that well-known piece of anonymous writing entitled "Footprints." Although so well-known it is worth recording again:

FOOTPRINTS

One night a man had a dream. He dreamed he was walking along the beach with the Lord. Across the sky flashed scenes from his life. For each scene he noticed two sets of footprints in the sand; one belonging to him, and the other to the Lord.

When the last scene of his life flashed before him he looked back at the footprints in the sand. He noticed that many times along the path of his life there was only one set of footprints. He also noticed that it happened at the very lowest and saddest times of his life. This really bothered him and he questioned the Lord about it: "Lord, you said that once I decided to follow you, you'd walk with me all the way. But I have noticed that during the most troublesome times in my life, there is only one set of footprints. I don't understand why, when I needed you most, you would leave me."The Lord replied: "My precious, precious child, I love you and I would never leave you. During your times of trial and suffering, when you see only one set of footprints, it was then that I carried you."

Relationship problems, often buried and unresolved for years, need to be healed as with Jeremy and Jo. Time does not heal of its own accord. Regularly we get elderly people come to Harnhill with various needs and frequently the root problem will go back to childhood and often involves relationships.

An Air Vice Marshall in his eighties writes: "On the first occasion I came to stay I benefited greatly from prayer counselling from Isabel and John. I was freed from a wrong relationship in childhood that has in fact affected my whole life." He continues to come to Harnhill occasionally to stay or sometimes on the Friday morning healing service when he often brings someone else.

Another woman, Rosa, of similar age or older, was told of Harnhill and its disabled room by someone at her church. Her daughter Coral has brought her twice and has already booked for next year. Rosa says: "The people we met there were so kind and thoughtful .... the food was really good. The days were spread out so that as well as enjoying ourselves we learnt a lot. We were not tired. But there was something different to do each day. I had two counsellors who helped me on two different days. Things I had worried about for many years. I was able to open up and get off my chest. I felt clear and cleansed which did me so much good; I felt a new woman."

I am conscious of not having addressed the terrible divisions and conflicts between nations across the world or between one faction or another within nations. But I would say of the remarkable reconciliations between nations or factions that I have been glad to witness, they have happened when one or more individuals on either side of the conflict have come together in agreement and then persuaded their fellows. Sometimes one or more of those individuals have first needed to find peace in his or her own heart before being able to approach the opponent. Inner peace and healing is the subject of the next chapter.

Man and Himself

The disobedience of Adam and Eve in the garden of Eden broke the perfect harmony in that peaceful and special place. It broke the relationship with God and also with each other. Also the man and the woman were no longer at peace and harmony in themselves. They were immediately conscious of being naked, which had not worried them previously. "They knew that they were naked and sewed fig leaves together to make themselves aprons" (Gen. 3v7). "When they heard the sound of the Lord God walking in the garden they hid themselves among the trees of the garden." (Gen. 3v8)

Adam and Eve knew shame and guilt for the first time. Shame and guilt are a great problem for mankind, a major factor in peoples' dis-ease. Shame and guilt rob us of our inner peace and often lead to illness of one sort or another, as well as conflict with other people and with God. Jesus by taking upon Himself all the consequences of our sin and disobedience on the cross and rising victorious over them restores our personal peace and harmony and health.

Jan, in leading the opening worship of one of our Wednesday evening healing services in Lent, spoke of the horror of the Cross and added: "Yet the Cross is the place where death is exchanged for life, where sickness is exchanged for health; where sorrow is exchanged for joy. The place where the love of God is most fully demonstrated." She might also have said: "The Cross is where shame and guilt are exchanged for inner peace and harmony."

Week by week at Harnhill we see the exchange happen, helped by the teaching of the good news of the Gospel. One way in which this is presented is through the "Circle of God's Love." A circle can be thought of as representing God's perfect love as it was manifested at the Creation with everything in perfect harmony. Adam and Eve felt secure within their circle of perfect love. Their disobedience shattered that perfection and they no longer felt safe, secure, loved, fear-free and at peace. That is the situation in which we find ourselves now in our fallen world. That is the state of most of our guests who arrive at Harnhill for help.

Our brokenness can be thought of under four main headings: Wounds, Sin, Bondages and the Enemy (occult).

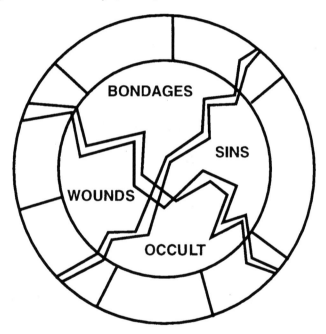

Circle of Brokenness

Wounds and hurts are often received in childhood as well as later in life. They may come through condemning words like: "You are useless" or "You will never be any good" or they may come through hurtful actions such as being deliberately tipped out of a pram by an elder brother, or set on by fellow pupils at school.

Such wounds and hurts can fester inside and lead to sinful desires of revenge and retaliation. But sin can come in many other ways as through greed, selfishness, lust and pride as with Eve.

Bondages too can come in different ways, the hurtful words received in childhood about being a failure can lead us into accepting that lie for ourselves rather than the truth that we are made in the image of God and precious. Other bondages can come through patterns of behaviour inherited from family or school. For many years after I was married we had to celebrate Christmas in exactly the same way as my parents had, even though this pattern was no longer convenient for our changed circumstances. To me that was the right way and I was in bondage to that pattern. It was some years before I recognised this bondage and was freed from it. Bondages can apply to much more serious things like patterns of behaviour in crime, abuse, perversion.

Then bondage, sins and wounds can be the means by which Satan enters our lives and uses our brokenness to manipulate us for his purposes. He can lead us into occult practices, disruptive behaviour, oppression and an unbalanced life. "But thanks be to God, who gives us the victory through Our Lord Jesus Christ." (1 Cor. 15v57)

Through Christian prayer counselling at Harnhill or elsewhere these things in our lives can be revealed to us by the Holy Spirit and healed through Christ and His Cross and Resurrection; the wounds are healed, the sins forgiven, the bondages broken and Satan defeated and banished. We then know for ourselves the truths prophesied by David in Psalm 103 and that proclaimed by Isaiah 43v4: "You are precious and honoured in my sight and I love you." When we truly experience this truth it gives us a wonderful joyous freedom and close relationship with Jesus, "abiding in Him and He in us."

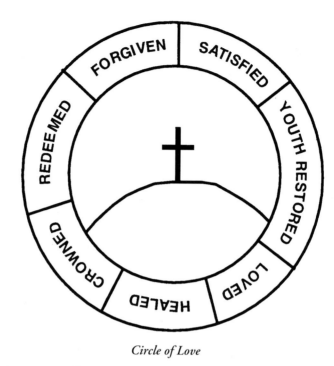

Circle of Love

The following stories illustrate and testify to these truths:

Debbie is a person who needed deliverance and the healing of Jesus in all the areas mentioned in the Circle of Love:

"Ten years ago in 1989 I became a Christian in the midst of the trauma of a broken marriage. The pain of rejection was excruciating. I had been left to bring up two young children, the youngest was only ten months old. This meant the start of my Christian Life was an uphill struggle, as I battled against bitterness and anger in my own strength. Release in the Holy Spirit came when I went to a church which ministered in the gifts of the Spirit. Here I received ministry for past involvement in occult activity. The Lord Jesus started a restoration process which reached a pinnacle when I became very depressed in 1995. I knew I needed help so I went to stay at Harnhill for a prayer and counselling weekend. I continued to come back for counselling over a six month period. During this time The Lord worked powerfully to set me free from past hurts and from the consequences of myself and family being deeply involved with faith healing, ouija boards, consulting mediums and astrology. I came away feeling like I had been through a personal spring clean! Praise the Lord for his goodness. At last I knew the peace which passes understanding."

"The healing process is often compared to peeling the skins of an onion. Just when you think it's completed the Lord reveals another layer. This happened to me two years ago. I had recognised the limits of my own ability to love others freely and very often felt condemned. I also had recurrent back pain, which had led me to give up nursing five years earlier. I came to see Arthur and Letty for prayer counselling. During the prayer Arthur had a word from the Lord to say my back would be healed and I would be able to nurse again. I had such a strong revelation of God's love for me. Now two years on the Lord has shown me the cause of the back pain and how to overcome it. I do believe it will be totally healed in his perfect timing. So much so after much prayer I have decided to take a Return to Nursing Course next Spring. I thank God for His faithful servants who minister in His Name at the Harnhill Centre."

Wendy, too, received wonderful healing and restoration from Jesus through the ministry at Harnhill: "It would be no exaggeration if I were to say that prior to July 1996, wild horses would not have been able to get me to go anywhere near Harnhill! I did not want anything to do with any Christians!"

"I was in deep trouble on 25th July 1996 and a visit to my Doctor in tears the next day was a most amazing divine intervention. He identified some problems in my early life and BELIEVED me. I walked out of the surgery with a smile and felt ten feet tall!"

"I returned to see my Christian Doctor friend a couple of days later, when he suggested that I would need psychotherapy, maybe a trip to Ireland to see a professor of Psychiatry, a visit to the Cheltenham psychiatrist and maybe a visit to Harnhill!"

"I was really praying, really praying after about 35 years of just speaking to a distant God in times of trouble. I knew that He was really with me and felt His love. "Nothing shall separate us from the love of God" (Romans 8:39) "I asked him to be with me for the rest of my life and to heal me of my mental illness. He has done that!"

"I phoned Harnhill one morning and was absolutely amazed when Mary Sanders spoke to me with such empathy. I told her my ghastly story and she responded so gently and quietly that I knew my desperate prayers were going to be answered. "

"My Counsellors were hand-picked by God: Jane and Liz. My first appointment was arranged speedily. Jane soon pinpointed the areas of importance, explained what form the counselling would take if, firstly, the Psychiatrist agreed and secondly, if I felt 'it was for me.' I knew it was, but felt I needed to take it to the Lord in prayer and really could not wait to get started!"

"I saw the Psychiatrist the next day. He listened intently when I told him all, particularly when I said I had contemplated suicide but now I felt that God had turned the situation right round and I knew that He would heal me. "I would like to have my counselling, please" I said. "Then you must be a Christian" he replied. "I certainly am and this is the first time in 35 years that I have been happy to tell anybody," I said.

"You go to Harnhill for your counselling. You have my blessing, they get better results than we do"

"Jane was so pleased when I told her and so they got started! I remember Jane asked me when I was converted. I told her that it was when I was about 10 and after hearing Billy Graham. This was incorrect, I knew Jesus was my personal friend and Saviour at the age of three! My ayah in Kenya, Mary Njoke confirmed this when I revisited the land of my birth in 1990. She said she simply told me about Jesus and I welcomed Him into my life."

"My love for him ran cold when I was 18, but that love is on fire for Him again 'since he met me at my point of dire need' at Harnhill in 1996. Jane really got to the root of my problems so quickly and because of all the prayers offered up for me and by me things progressed really fast. I never missed one single session although there were days when I had to ask for grace to overcome Satan and his forces for evil. Jane had said at the beginning that the counselling would be much more effective for a Christian and that was true."

"I climbed up into the loft and got my beautiful Bible down. It was in good condition after being up there for 30+ years except that it smelt a bit musty. As I got it down I thought: "I am going to read it so much now that it will get such an airing that it will lose that smell for ever." With constant use the smell vanished and, even more exciting, the verses I knew by heart came flooding back to my memory. I had forgotten just how much I knew and the references too! The first verse I recalled was Romans 8 verse 28: "All things work together for good to them that love God, to them who are called according to his purpose." I fell to my knees, cried and thanked him for saving me from the self-destruction I had planned only days before."

"My regular visits to see my G.P were truly amazing, he helped me to start rebuilding my life and at each visit encouraged me so much. He suggested that I should borrow his copy of *Desert Harvest* by Arthur Dodds. I found it immensely helpful. Nearly all the verses of Scripture in the book are ones that are specially meaningful to me e.g. 2 Cor. 12v9: "And He said unto me, My grace is sufficient for thee: for my strength is made perfect in weakness. Most gladly therefore will I rather glory in my infirmities that the Power of Christ may rest upon me." So often I have been able to identify with Paul's actions and attitudes, that I am really looking forward to greeting him when I get to heaven."

"I began to commit everything to him, just as I had done before and to trust him and to obey. Suddenly I loved my life and was free from my burdens. I never missed a Wednesday night healing service and often went on Fridays too. I always found that the Lord had a word or a picture for me and I did not seem to have any problem going for prayer ministry. I remember one particular time when I went to Letty and Arthur Dodds and fell straight back onto the floor with such a thud, resting in the Holy Spirit that Arthur burst out laughing and I was amazed that I had not hurt myself! I attended an Alpha Course and I joined a church, encouraged all along by Jane and Liz who I believe 'prepared the ground' so to speak."

"One day I thought it would be good to join a Saturday course, especially as I was assured that Suzanne and Frank were fun people! That was definitely the case! I knew as soon as I booked that this Saturday Jesus was going to have the rest of my life. It was October 26th 1996 in the Barn. Frank and Suzanne are my kind of people! I chose a rather prominent place in the front row which was so unlike me!"

"Frank started the day with a great welcome, a vibrant smiling 'on fire for the Lord' type of person, with a great sense of humour. I just knew that he had been hand-picked for me on that particular day. Thank you Lord! Some of the things he said are so clear in my memory that he could have said them yesterday. He started with an illustration of "growing." In the Middle East they plant the Chinese Bamboo. For the first four years they water and fertilise the plants with no signs of growth. In the fifth year they again water and fertilise the plants and in five weeks the bamboo grows 90 feet. Did it grow 90 feet in five years or five weeks? The answer is of course five years. I felt that this portrayed the way the Lord had been working in my Spiritual Life. I had been at my worst at the end of July and in three months I had grown 90 feet! Frank's hand-out was excellent. He gave us twelve names for God e.g. Elohim, Adonai, El Shaddai, Jehovah Jireh. He then suggested that we each choose a name that best suited our need or experience. I looked at the list and quickly decided that Jehovah Rophe ("The Lord that Heals" – Exodus 15v26) was the name for me. Next Frank suggested that we should each pray either silently or out loud, in tongues or in whichever way we wanted. I just prayed out loud: "Oh Lord, please let me pray in tongues, I have never done that and I would love to do that now!" Suddenly I just opened my mouth and these words came pouring out! They were not words I had ever uttered before, sort of guttural and so fast like Arabic. I only knew that they were to do with inner healing, something I had longed for. Then I heard His still small voice say: 'I am the Lord that healeth Thee.' My simple response was straight from my heart: 'Thank you father.' "And I was made whole from that hour."

In addition to the Gospel teaching given to the residents who stay at the Harnhill Centre and to those who come to training days, we also receive Gospel Truths in the healing Services on Wednesday evenings or Friday mornings. One of the Biblical Truths we most need to take on board is that of self-acceptance. Barry Smith, a Trustee and a businessman preached on this subject one Friday morning recently:

ACCEPTANCE

Picture this scene–

Michael came home from school, really miserable.

"What's the problem?" said Granddad.

"Well I can never get any friends. I've tried all term. When I ask people at school if I can join in, and keep following them about, they just tell me to clear off."

"Michael, you're special, and you need to realise that people will want to be with you when you are happy with yourself."

"You are desperate, and that makes them feel you're a bit of a loser which puts them off."

"Why don't we plan some new hobbies? You'll forget about feeling left out – you'll feel better about yourself – life's full of interesting things and you will make lots of friends that way."

"Will it work?"

"Let's try it and see."

The core dynamics of the playground never go away. They are simply buried under a veneer of respectability when we become adults – sometimes hardly buried at all.

The simple principle here is so true – but sometimes seems to be beyond attainment.

If we are at peace with ourselves, not always seeking approval or attention or trying to prove ourselves, we are likely to have more successful relationships.

Others are comfortable with people who are comfortable with themselves. This is all about self-acceptance.

What is self-acceptance? It's confidence. It breeds humility, security, self-esteem, self-respect. The opposite is attention-seeking, guilt, self-loathing, depression, inadequacy, insecurity. People who have difficulty with self-acceptance can be introverts, like victims expecting the next blow. Or hype themselves up with attention-seeking attitudes, attention-seeking behaviour that usually alienates other people.

But we need to develop a strength within, that is not dependent upon others or on their approval or affirmation, or what we achieve or how we look. Of course, our society often derides self-rejection – achievement or appearance are taught as being so important. Some people are in a terrible trap, a self-perpetuating vicious circle; spending their whole lives picking up worthless crumbs of approval, striving to achieve in order to be accepted. I was like this for years, until I became a Christian – maybe I am still to some extent. But if we are secure in ourselves, in who we are, we are far more likely to generate acceptance and respect. What a paradox!

But you know the Good News don't you, before I tell you? As Christians, we have the answer. If there's one thing that God never wanted for the human race, it was insecurity. Jesus accepts anyone who turns to Him, including the despised, the outcast, the sinner.

This truth should give you the encouragement, the assurance, the confidence, the security, the acceptance the world cannot have. Indeed, if we cannot appreciate this truth, – that God is a God of grace and unconditional love, who accepts us as we are – we are not accepting Him as He is!

See yourself as God sees you. Not only does He accept you as you are. He sees you as you can be, and it's His unconditional love that enables you to accept yourself as you are. Then see yourself as you are going to be!

If we believe God accepts us just as we are, it follows that God accepts others as they are.

This lack of acceptance results in us being very judgmental of others and finding it difficult to accept them.

Many of us applaud Jesus' acceptance of the robber on the cross yet we cannot accept our neighbours.

Acceptance by God means that we can acknowledge in honesty our own strengths and weaknesses and at the same time, have a loving concern for the welfare and feelings of others and accept others as they are.

So love yourself and accept yourself and accept others because God does not make junk!

Isaiah 43v4 says "You are precious and honoured in my sight." Yes, God does not make junk.

Lack of self acceptance is the refusal to see ourselves as God sees us and we need to repent of that."

Self-acceptance and self-worth are something with which the young often have difficulty:

A teenage son had walked out of school in deep depression, wanting to have nothing to do with any of his peers, spending most of his time at home tearfully, watching television, sleeping or going out wherever his parents went, being comfortable only with older people and not wanting anything to do with people of his own age. This went on for a number of months, having a noticeably negative effect on the home life of the family concerned.

The young man came for prayer counselling at Harnhill and after the third session, the parents noticed a marginal improvement in the general demeanour of their son. A week after this third counselling session. the young man went up to his father, hugged him and said: "I am so happy. I'm all right. All the negative feelings I had about myself and the concern that I had nothing to look forward to apart from sixty years of misery have gone." When asked how this came about. He said the following: "Last Monday, the lady prayed for me, that God would put all these negative thoughts at the back of my mind. She said to me 'and He will.' Then something happened that I can't explain, but I have been fine ever since. I didn't want to mention it before, in case I woke up one morning and I was back where I was; but it's now six days since the lady prayed for me and it's just got better and better and better each day.' The father commented that his son is smiling now in a way he had never done before!"

We have already noted that God loves to heal us and wants us to come to self-acceptance not just for our own benefit, but that we may fulfil His purpose for us and be a blessing to others.

A judge writes:

"When we first came to Harnhill in 1993 we immediately identified with the warmth of its welcome and the real presence of the Holy Spirit pervading all that was going on. What particularly impressed us was the informality both in terms of worship and administration, and the evident trusting that the Holy Spirit was in charge, directing everything. This seemed to create an atmosphere in which the Holy Spirit was welcomed and 'allowed' to move freely in the lives of those involved in running the house and of course the visitors."

"Wednesday evening healing services in the barn were well attended and made a deep impression on us. The Word was spoken with such conviction. We started to attend day courses on a variety of important topics, and learned so much. We heard about this Texan evangelist called Clay McLean, and our first experience of hearing Clay and Mary speak was a complete revelation. We had seldom heard anyone speak with quite such authority before."

"In 1994 we came to a residential few days entitled: 'Time Aside with Jesus,' and experienced even more the love and peace which Harnhill offers. A little later, Arthur organised an Alpha Course at Harnhill, and yet again we were on our learning curve, and being equipped to assist with and lead Alpha Courses elsewhere."

"We have continued to attend courses and teaching opportunities at Harnhill over the years, and have learned so much."

"Harnhill has a team of people dedicated to counselling those with deep hurts. As a family we have all been, and continue to be, blessed by this aspect of the ministry of this very special place."

He and his wife have also helped in various ways at Harnhill and occasionally, as a family, have led the worship for the Wednesday healing service.

I have known Joan H. for over twenty years. She received considerable healing from Jesus and then became part of our healing ministry team while Letty and I were still in our parish. When the Harnhill Centre opened she became part of the outer team, ministering at Healing Services, became a prayer counsellor and also a Trustee. She writes, "Little did I realise that my twelve years' close association with Harnhill was preparing me so well for the job I do now. Over the years I had lapped up and leant many aspects of the healing ministry by attending the valuable training days and teaching courses at the Centre. All the time my personal walk with Jesus was becoming more important as I progressed along a path of healing in body, mind and spirit."

"Harnhill is also keen to further the work of evangelism, particularly through the Alpha Course. I was drawn into helping in this too. One day in 1997 whilst helping to lead an Alpha Conference at Harnhill I met the Regional Organiser. He simply said: 'There is a job for you at St Matthew's Church in Cheltenham if you would like it. I was amazed! The job was to be responsible for prayer ministry in the church and to encourage and train a ministry team. To be available for personal prayer ministry, to encourage personal and corporate prayer and to lead the House Groups. To help with Alpha and to be part of the staff team in everything. I did not realise until later that it was a paid job with a house thrown in!"

"Fortunately I retired early from teaching, was offering myself for ordination and was wanting a change of church. Also my husband worked in Cheltenham. How amazing and gracious the Lord is. His timing is perfect."

"I suddenly realised I was equipped for the job, thanks to Harnhill, but I wanted to be sure and asked the Lord for specific guidance. It had to be obvious enough for me to trip over! He gave me three specific signs and I knew it was right. Now I have been there three and a half years in the job and am about to be ordained. I love the work and am so grateful to the Lord and Harnhill for equipping me. It was Adrian Plass who said: 'You just can't trust God!' I know now what he means."

Another person who was helped to receive her healing at Harnhill was Joan P. She was then able to minister to others:

"I began to suffer bouts of depression when I was a teenager. On the surface I was seemingly outgoing and assured but underneath there was a blackness that was underpinned by fear. I daren't watch news on TV. I was scared to be alone in the dark and frightened of so many things. The depressions continued into adulthood. I suffered post-natal depression but the worst depression came in my early forties."

"This time not only my mind but my body was affected. I couldn't climb the stairs without resting halfway up and I was beginning to have severe panic attacks when I fought for breath and often collapsed. Eventually I came to a full stop. I had to have six months away from teaching, a time of which I have no memory at all. I was taking maximum doses of tranquilisers and anti-depressants. In other words, I was a complete mess."

"At this point a friend gave me a leaflet for Harnhill. I plucked up enough courage to phone the Centre and I arrived the following day. For some time I had been unable to face a room of adults. I couldn't go into a shop without a panic attack and coping with strangers was an impossibility. As I came through the door of Harnhill the peace met me. It felt like coming home. I was surrounded by Christian love and tender care and I met Christ in a way that I hadn't known since I was a little girl."

"It would be lovely to say that my healing was immediate but I had too many channels blocked by things like fear, guilt and anger. However I came for prayer many times and after much prayer ministry I received my healing. The strange thing was that my prayer ministry ran side by side with my psychiatrist's care and there was never a conflict between the two. My psychiatrist had the expertise to find the roots of the problem but it was Harnhill who put the prayer and peace into a difficult time."

"The real difference in me was that now for the first time in my life I had inner peace and a joy that was always there even on the darkest days. I was no longer alone and with God I stopped being fearful. Many years have passed and I have never suffered from depression again. I have a new life in Christ."

"When I was better, I felt very deeply that I was being called by God to minister to others. I trained to be an Anglican Reader but no sooner was I licensed than I knew God was calling me to train for ordination. Last year I was priested by my Bishop in my own village church where I now minister. It was wonderful to have the Harnhill Warden as one of the priests to lay hands on me at that ordination. One of the great privileges of my life was the day I was allowed to celebrate communion in the Friday morning healing service at Harnhill."

"I have been so blessed by Harnhill and I only pray that I am able to pass on some of that blessing to others."

Pain

One of the manifestations of man's not being right with himself is the experience of pain and suffering. It is one of the results of the disobedience of Adam and Eve, and the continued disobedience of mankind. Not that individual sin brings automatically pain and suffering. Often the reverse seems to be the case. Rather we are all caught up in a fallen world and often it seems that the godly are asked to transform the suffering to good and to God's glory with His help. Jesus infers this in John 9v1-3: "As He passed by, He saw a man blind from his birth. And His disciple asked Him 'Rabbi, who sinned, this man or his parents?' Jesus answered: 'It was not that this man sinned, or his parents, but that the works of God might be made manifest in him.' "

Pain comes in all manner of ways. Separation often brings pain as with the little boy who arrives at his boarding school for the first time and waves goodbye to his mother as she drives away and he tries unsuccessfully to keep back the tears. Or the pain of the little girl who hears her father storming out of the house for good after yet another angry quarrel with her mother. Then there is the pain of separation as the husband says goodbye to his wife and goes off to war. Or the pain of rejection at any age and the pain of loneliness. The pain of loss and bereavement. More obviously there is the pain of an accident or illness or disability with its accompanying frustration and immobility. Life can be full of a great deal of pain which Satan loves to use to make us resentful and bitter or at any rate full of self-pity: "Poor old me." But just as Satan seeks to use our pain to his own ends God can use it even more greatly for our benefit and that of others and for His glory. We cannot calculate how many thousands of people have been helped by Paul because of his "thorn in the flesh."

Although this thorn in the flesh is described as "a messenger of Satan," nevertheless it is "given." The giver, by implication, is God. This concept is found elsewhere in the Bible. God is sovereign and rules over all. Satan can only operate as permitted by God as in the first two chapters of the Book of Job. So although we may be afflicted by pain, suffering or misfortune to the delight of Satan, yet God can turn these setbacks to good and work out His purpose through them to our benefit, the benefit of others and to the greater glory of God, if we will co-operate with Him in our pain. Joni Erickson is a notable example of this. Her terrible accident, disability and pain, have been the means of her drawing closer to Jesus than most of her contemporaries and have inspired and encouraged countless thousands of us, all to the Glory of God.

The thorn in the flesh was both "the messenger of Satan to harass" Paul and also the means by which God kept him humble and not "too elated;" the means by which he taught Paul: "My grace is sufficient for you" or as the Good News Bible translates it: "My grace is all you need." That translation goes on to say "my power is strongest when you are weak" (2 Cor. 12v7-10). This truth has encouraged thousands of Christians including myself.

Mr Gaius Davies, a senior London consultant psychiatrist, when speaking at Harnhill, said: "It seems that God allows the adversary (Satan) to afflict us, but He also offers to be with us in the midst of our suffering to help us with all sorts of victories for Him, if we permit it."

During many years of pastoral visiting I have been amazed at the radiance and victory apparent in many little-known house-bound "saints." In spite of their pain and disabilities or, should I say, because of their pain and disabilities, their faces have shone and glowed with their faith in and love for Jesus: an inspiration and example to any who have met them. I have come away from these people humbled, encouraged and inspired. The times I have felt closest to Jesus have been in illness and pain; but also when looking at a beautiful seascape or landscape from the top of a mountain on my own; gazing at a sunset or evening sky full of stars; when praying with someone in need; or in hard times. The most meaningful Christmas I ever spent was in a prisoner-of-war camp in the second world war, not the wonderful ones I have had with my family at home. In prison camp I lay on a wooden bed without any of the usual Christmas trimmings and especially bereft of family and home. But as I lay there in my loneliness I suddenly felt very, very close to Jesus. I was able to identify myself, as never before or since, with the poverty, humility and vulnerability of the infant babe in a grubby stable in an enemy-occupied country.

In times of illness and pain I have most often been conscious of God speaking to me through the Holy Spirit. This book would not have been written if it were not for the repeated chest infections which affected my heart and caused total exhaustion so that for many months it was an effort to drag myself a few steps. In consequence I could not accept any of the many invitations to speak and minister in various places far and wide and had to cancel those appointments already made. At some point in my illness and weakness I asked the Lord what He was trying to say to me in this situation. He said: "Write another book of some of the things you would talk about if you were able to accept those invitations." Here it is.

However, I cannot in all honesty, yet fully, identify with James who, at the beginning of his epistle, says: "Count it all joy .... when you meet various trials." I more readily agree with John Wimber's song "O give Him all your tears and sadness, give Him all your years of pain and you'll enter into life in Jesus' name." And I can agree with C.S Lewis who, if I remember correctly, says in his book The Problem of Pain: "God often uses pain as a megaphone to shout at us when we are hard of hearing." There seems to be an implication there that it would be sensible for us to be more attentive to His voice when we are well.

Pain often comes unexpectedly and by various means beyond our control. One of the most common causes of pain and sadness is bereavement. Marcia, the artist who painted the picture on the cover of this book, after a visit to the Harnhill Centre which she calls the 'Love Health Farm of Healing,' wrote: "How glad I was when Jane Chichester advised me to go to Harnhill when I lost my mother and not to go somewhere for physical pampering which I thought I needed. What I really needed was to know the faith through His Son dying for our sins on the Cross and carrying all our past and present and so to get better through prayer and the work of the Holy Spirit. This is what happened and I am so grateful to Harnhill, a haven of trust, peace and renewal which sends us out again into the world to be a strong light for Him." She and her husband Robin, who subsequently came to Harnhill, have indeed been strong lights for Him. It was not long before they were leading an Alpha Course in their home and generally witnessing for Him in their area.

A moving story of suffering and bereavement is told by a former member of the Harnhill staff, Diane. It concerns her husband Peter, a Fleet Air Arm pilot, who suffered greatly with cancer. Diane says:

"I became a Christian when my daughter prayed for me and then my heart's desire was for my husband to love the Lord Jesus and for eight years I prayed for that and tried so hard to win him to the Lord. I often felt that he would never change. Then one day my daughter said "You can't change other people, you will have to change yourself." So I concentrated on getting myself right with God. My husband's attitude softened and he encouraged me more in my work with the church."

"Then came Mission England. I was privileged to be a counsellor at Ashton Gate and was thrilled to see how God worked there. Peter refused to come with me. One Sunday, when I was out at Pathfinders, Peter turned on the television and watched a Mission England meeting in Birmingham. When I arrived home he said:

'I prayed the prayer with Billy Graham and asked Jesus into my heart.' I was filled with joy and over the next sixteen months watched Peter's faith grow. At first he said it wasn't necessary for him to go to church to be a Christian. But then a friend put Peter's name forward for prayer healing at her church and Peter began to come to church regularly with me."

"During his illness Peter's faith grew but it was difficult to watch him suffer over the last two and a half months when he changed beyond recognition. When he was in hospital and nearly died he had a vision of the Lord Jesus. He told me the Lord was standing with his arms out, smiling at him. He said he felt complete assurance of forgiveness of his sins and was very happy. The Lord Jesus was with us both during that time of Peter's suffering. All our prayers for help and strength were answered. He was with us during our walk through the valley of the shadow of death and He comforted us."

"Peter was very brave in his suffering and I know he is with Our Lord and is safe. God has granted my heart's desire for Peter to know and love the Lord Jesus but now I have to continue my earthly journey without him. When it hurts too much Jesus is there. I know He understands and loves me. When I was driving to hospital one day when Peter was desperately ill, I felt I couldn't bear it. Then it was as if Jesus was with me saying: 'I know how you feel; I know what it is like to suffer; I suffered for your sake because I love you.' That is still true."

I first met Diane a few months later when she joined a party I was leading to the Holy Land. She told me her story as we walked from one biblical site to another. On return to England she began coming to Harnhill and helping. A year or so later she joined the permanent staff at the Centre. Her radiant personality drew guests to the love of Jesus. It was as though her suffering had been turned into winsomeness for Jesus. In her one saw the truth of Nettie Rose's words in her song: "Praise you Lord for the wonder of your healing .... the path of pain is hallowed, for your love has made it sweet .... turned our thorns to roses .... they bloom upon your brow."

The Lord blessed Diane's ministry at Harnhill. Typical of it is an incident when she was looking after the guests one Thursday evening, she recalls:

"Tessa had told me that she loved singing but was now very deaf in one ear. We were having prayer for healing and I felt we should pray for Tessa to be healed of her deafness. The two people nearest Tessa put their hands on her head and we all held hands and prayed for her to be healed. When I saw her the next day she told me that when she woke that morning she heard the birds singing. Then she

Diane barbecueing at Harnhill

realised she was lying on her good ear! She said later that she had received about 80% of her hearing in the bad ear." Very often it seems that those whom the Lord has helped through pain and suffering are then used by Him to help others.

Ivan and Patricia moved from Coventry to Cirencester in order to be able to help at Harnhill as members of the Outer Team. She writes:

"My first contact with Harnhill was in February 1990 when Isabel asked us to come to give our testimony during a 'Time Aside.' The subject was bereavement; our fourth child had lived only a day and through that experience we became Christians. In addition Ivan suffered the bereavement of not being employed and the loss of his high-powered job."

"We arrived at Harnhill on the Monday evening to be ready for the Tuesday. Breakfast in bed is normal for guests at Harnhill and Wyn brought ours singing as she came. As we started to eat tears ran down my face – I was so overwhelmed by God's love for me – it was very precious – it was His presence alone. I said I didn't know God loved me so much! It was that experience which led me to know His heart more deeply. I realised that Harnhill was where the love of God was known, where the Holy Spirit was welcomed and where the Lord was blessed. Although we were already involved with Prayer Ministry for Healing in Coventry I am so grateful for the privilege of coming to serve the Lord at Harnhill; of knowing his equipping; of seeing people freed to be themselves; of seeing the gifts of the Spirit operating in big and small ways, bringing Jesus' victory over Satan into reality in everyday living."

Sometimes people carry the pain of traumatic memories and guilt with them into old age. Jeremy, who appears with his golf clubs in chapter 5, was holding a barbecue for his wife's family. Among those who came was an older man who we will call Brian. He drank a lot and seemed sad and in need of help. Jeremy went over to him in the garden and asked him what was troubling him. Brian told him that since the war every night he had a recurring nightmare of the Normandy landings where his brother was killed on the beach. Ever since he had carried this guilt of "Why my brother and not me?" Before Brian left Jeremy asked if he could pray with him. He asked God to lift this traumatic memory and burden of guilt from him and give him a good night's sleep. God worked and stopped his nightmare and started to move in Brian's life. The day after the party Brian rang up Jeremy to thank him and tell him he had slept the night through for the first time since Normandy. Jeremy said this incident brought home to him what many elderly people had gone through in the war which he and younger generations did not understand.

Another elderly person, Renee, a woman in her eighties has been coming to Harnhill off and on for some years. Her problem is angina which greatly restricted her. She received prayer with the laying on of hands for healing. Now she is able to make her way up and down stairs without difficulty. Angina pains are unpleasant as I know.

Another pensioner who experienced very serious heart problems and spent some time in intensive care at the Gloucester Royal Hospital was Edwin. He was encouraged by Mrs Rebbic and his Vicar to come to Harnhill. A parishioner drove him arriving about 3 pm on the Monday. He writes:

"I was feeling very tired and weary and experiencing breathing difficulties and needed to rely heavily on the support of my walking stick. After a short rest, events proceeded according to the prescribed programme. Tuesday was relatively normal. I took part in all the activities until it was time to retire for the night. At that point my health began to deteriorate so much that I thought I would have to call for an ambulance. However I turned to the Bible for words of wisdom and comfort. I read most of the night, mostly from St John's Gospel. In the early morning I put my Bible aside and laid my heavy head on the pillow and tried to sleep. It was at that point I became convinced that the Lord was commanding me to get up and walk as in St John 5v8. I did get up and walk (without taking up my bed as in the Gospel story!) and became aware that my breathing was more natural and my angina pains had subsided. I felt so elated that I gazed up into the heavens with raised hands thanking and praising Jesus incessantly. I was so exhilarated I felt like waking up all the staff and residents to join me in my thanks and praise. With tear-stained face and joy in my heart I returned to my bed noticing it was now 5 o'clock. I soon fell asleep to be woken up by John with breakfast soon after 8 am."

"After dressing I walked to the lounge without my stick and joined the rest for the usual praise and worship at the start of the day. I asked the leader if I might make an announcement. I tried to share with them the joy of my experience and the awesomeness of the closeness of Jesus. However the message was understood, it was joyously received. I returned home full of joy and peace, almost leaving my walking stick behind. My wife and family could not believe the change that had taken place in such a short time."

I met him two and a half years later still full of life.

Those who come to Harnhill are not all healed physically or even freed from their pain, but they seldom, if ever, do not receive some blessing. It is wonderful when they do receive physical healing as well as release from all their fear, and trauma and pain. The next story is such a case.

John, a doctor and Pam his wife write:

"About six years ago we were ministering at the end of a Wednesday healing service when a girl of about 35 came to us for ministry in floods of tears. She was so upset that she was unable to tell us what she wanted us to pray for. We both prayed quietly in tongues and after a while she was able to tell us that she had had cancer of the breast for some years, had had radiotherapy and chemotherapy for it, but despite the treatment the cancer had continued to spread and now involved her bones, liver and lungs. That day she had been to see her hospital consultant and he had told her there was nothing else he could do and that she had only three months to live. She had two children and a lovely husband and she did not want to die. She had come to Harnhill in desperation, from a long way away, hoping for a miracle of healing."

"We felt devastated and prayed very simple prayers giving her to the Lord and asking Him to heal her in His mercy. Six months later we were again ministering at a Wednesday evening healing service and already praying with somebody. We saw a girl whom we did not recognise come and sit near us obviously wanting to come to us for prayer. When we finished praying with our first client, we called her over. She said: 'You won't remember me but I came to you six months ago and told you that I had cancer, and had been given only three months to live. I felt I must come back and tell you that I have just had my second completely clear 'whole body scan,' and that they say that I am completely well, and they can't understand it.' We joined her in thanking God rather enthusiastically."

Pam herself has since received wonderful healing and release from pain after an accident. She writes:

"We were walking on Tresco in the Isles of Scilly when I slipped and fell. I had terrible pain in my right knee and could not get up. Getting to the hospital on St Mary's, where we were staying, by golf buggy, boat and taxi, was a nightmare. The GP who examined me said that I had done severe damage to my knee and that he was admitting me for a week. However I was allowed to go home after two days, when we were due to leave. We went by ambulance to the helicopter, being lifted on and off and into our car."

"John got me home and into bed. After a scan and an x-ray the surgeon was very negative. He said that I had fractured the tibia, ruptured the cruciate ligament and the medial collateral ligament, torn the cartilage and there was a lot of bleeding into the joint. He said that it would be a year before I could walk normally, that arthritis was sure to set in, and that I would probably require a replacement knee joint. I felt that all this negativity was like a pronouncement or a curse, and I rejected it in Jesus' name. That evening I came to the Wednesday evening healing service at Harnhill and asked for ministry. I asked my prayer ministers to pray off the negativity and pronouncements or curse, which they did very powerfully. Then one of the prayer ministers asked if she could put her hand on my knee and they prayed for healing. I felt a surge of heat go through my knee. When they had finished praying I told them about the heat and the minister said that she had felt things moving under her fingers. I knew that I had received a blessing of healing."

"On the Sunday evening at a healing service at our church I went forward for prayer and I had a sensation of pins and needles starting at my hip and going down my right leg. I knew the Lord was at work again accelerating the healing. Three weeks later I had an arthroscopy when the surgeon looked inside the joint with an optical instrument. When I next saw him he seemed very surprised and said that it was all good news. The fracture site was smooth and healthy-looking, only one cruciate ligament was torn, he was happy with the position of other ligaments which should re-attach themselves, the cartilage was fine and he had found less arthritis than he would expect to find in a normal joint of my age. He said that I should be as right as rain by Christmas! The physiotherapist has been amazed at the speed of my progress. Eight weeks after the accident I had given up the wheelchair and the elbow crutches and after nine weeks I can now walk short distances unaided and I only use a stick on occasions."

On October 18th Pam walked 2 miles on the Long Mynd in Shropshire and the same distance the next day with no ill effects. Praise the Lord!

Some of us are not so fortunate as Pam in receiving complete release from our pain and healing of our disabilities. It would seem that St Paul was not, but like him we can learn from it and through it. I quote again 2 Cor. 12v7 to 10 (N.I.V) " .... There was given to me a thorn in my flesh, a messenger of Satan, to torment me. Three times I pleaded with the Lord to take it away from me. But He said to me, 'My grace is sufficient for you for my power is made perfect in weakness' therefore I will boast all the more gladly about my weaknesses, so that Christ's power may rest in me. That is why for Christ's sake, I delight in weakness, in insults, in hardships, in persecution, in difficulties. For when I am weak then I am strong."

We can usually learn from pain, become more dependent on the Lord and His Grace and can let it be used by Him to help others. Nevertheless I believe it is right to go on praying for healing, like blind Bartimaeus who 'cried out all the more' or like Jennifer Rees Larcombe who went on praying as well as learning but did not receive healing until after eight painful years in a wheelchair.

None of us will receive total wholeness of body, soul (i.e. mind, emotions, will) and spirit until we come to glory in heaven but our aim is perfection in Christ through the power of his Holy Spirit, perfect wholeness and harmony between God and mankind, man and man, man and himself, and mankind and the environment.

Man and his Environment

The fourth relationship that suffered as a result of Adam and Eve's disobedience, and which continues to suffer through men's and women's disobedience, is the relationship between mankind and the environment. God created everything beautiful, perfect and harmonious. Through disobedience that beauty is marred, the perfection shattered and the harmony destroyed. And the process continues. Christ came to restore that broken relationship as He did the other three, and the Christian concept of healing includes the restoration of this relationship as well as the other three.

"Through the Son then God decided to bring the whole universe back to Himself. God made peace through His Son's death on the cross and so brought back to Himself all things both in Heaven and on Earth." Colossians 1v20.

And so from time to time at Harnhill we have study days on the Healing of the Environment or similar titles. At one such day a few years ago we had two speakers who not only believe in this concept, but have sought to put it into practice: David Ursell and James More-Molyneux.

David and Susan Ursell were very much involved when we started the Harnhill Centre. Susan is the oldest daughter of Robert and Mary Henly, from whom we bought Harnhill Manor. David then managed the Manor Farm. The two of them helped in all sorts of ways during the first four years of the Centre's life. Then they went down to a small farm in North Devon. David has always been a champion of organic farming and now all produce on their Devon farm is organic. They are also great Christians and David has now trained and become a non-stipendiary priest of the Church of England. He is also involved in running a help-line for West Country farmers in their present desperate situation. A little while ago David produced a paper: "Treating the Land with Respect," which expressed some of his convictions. He writes:

"We do not need to have any greater incentive to treat the land with respect than Psalm 24v1: 'The Earth is the Lord's and everything in it.' Sadly the Christian record in this area is not all it could be. This world belongs to God and we must treat the land with all the respect of which we are capable. God calls us to have dominion over the Earth (Gen. 1v28), that is to manage it as God desires. From the beginning God's test for our relationship with the Creator was how we treated a certain tree (Gen. 3v7). 'You must not eat of the tree in the middle of the garden.' But they did eat and we know the consequences. Not before time people today are becoming more conscious of ecological sins. Environmental issues are central to the gospel and the well-being of mankind."

"One of the most famous verses in the Bible is John 3v16: 'For God so loved the world he gave His only begotten Son.' The Greek word for 'world' is 'cosmos'; that is everything that is in the world; the whole of God's creation about which He said: 'It is very good,' Gen 1v31. What an awesome responsibility to look after all that on God's behalf. We have a mandate from God to work with the natural world in the role of stewards. Stewards do not own the land, God does. But we are responsible to God for it. Stewards must use the resources at their disposal to the best possible advantage i.e. God's advantage. Jesus taught us like the prophets before Him that God is concerned for the poor. As the environment breaks down and the Earth produces less, the poor suffer most. Environmental destruction is a major cause of world famine. Jesus warned us stewards that we would have to give an account of our stewardship."

"We are entrusted with these resources of the Earth for a limited period. 43% of the Earth's land surface is already desert or semi-desert. A further 20% is under threat of desertification. We know that the Roman Empire used North Africa, much of which is now desert, to produce most of its wheat for making bread for its citizens. Here in Britain an area greater than Berkshire is lost every five years in urban and industrial development, land is not a replaceable commodity. It takes fifty years to produce half an inch (1.25 cm) of top soil by sensitive farming methods. No more land is being created; we desperately need to treat with respect what we have."

"As human beings, God had placed us in a unique position in the creation. We are set between God and Creation with the responsibility to care for the Earth. Philosophically we are the same as animals but morally and spiritually we are potentially divine. Nature is what God gives us to work with; culture is our response. Agriculture had a huge influence in bringing about civilisation. Once the land was cared for in one place, and could maintain existence for humans, then culture could begin. These systems that were produced were sustainable as indeed were the systems of production for thousands of years. Where the system was exploited and the soil not fed by returning organic matter then disaster struck as with the Sahara."

David Ursell then quotes Windell Berry who has said: "Destroy soil and the health of human communities follows. The strength of a farm is in its soil." David Ursell continues:

"The history of the Christian faith stems from a totally land-based people, and thankfully we have some very useful advice for natural farming techniques in the Bible. Countless verses give us instruction on how to treat our land, our animals, trees and plants and of course, one another. 'Woe to you who join house to house and field to field until there is no more space, and you are made to dwell alone in the midst of the land' (Isaiah, 5v8). Larger and larger units and more and more isolation and loneliness for farmers. 'When you lay siege to a city for a long time, fighting against it, do not destroy its trees by putting an axe to them because you can eat their fruit. Do not cut them down. Are the trees of the field people that you besiege them?' (Deut. 20v19). And again: 'When you reap the harvest of your land do not reap in the very edge of your fields' (Lev. 23v22). This ensured some was left for the poor in those days and is in contrast with today's practice of cropping and hence spraying fields right to the hedgerows which results in a loss of wildlife and the predators that assist control of disease in the crops." I am reminded of Oscar Colburn, a well-known Christian farmer in the Cotswolds, who made sure there was adequate room along the hedgerows for the pheasants and the wildlife to breed. At the same time he was a very successful farmer.

David Ursell continues: by quoting Lev. 26v34:

" 'The land will enjoy its Sabbath year too.' Continuous corn has meant high inputs of fertiliser and resultant run-off into the waterways. An increase in the use of pesticides has meant residues in water and a depletion in many forms of wildlife. Compare that with God's created ways:

'You care for the land and water it; you nourish it abundantly.

The streams of God are filled with water to provide the people with corn for so you have ordained it.

You drench its furrows and level its ridges; you soften it with showers and bless its crops.

You crown the year with its bounty and your carts overflow with abundance. The grasslands of the desert overflow; the hills are clothed with gladness.

The meadows are covered with flocks and the valleys are mantled with corn; they shout for joy and sing' (Psalm 65. 9 to 13). "

"How we treat our soil is of paramount importance. We are called to be fruitful and multiply and to replenish the Earth (Gen. 1v28). The top four inches of soil is what maintains our life here on Earth. We must care for it with all our might. Most criticism is levelled at farmers, but gardeners too need to be aware. More chemicals in the form of fertilisers and pesticides are used per acre in domestic gardens than ever is used in agriculture."

"One of the latest techniques that is entering our food chain is that of Genetically Modified Organisms. Potentially these plants and the production systems that they bring with them are very dangerous. So much so that no insurance companies will take on a bio-technological company. This generation may never see the full effects, but we must plead for our children's children and insist on labelling and make choices in our purchases. There are limits to the insults that the environment and especially the land can bear. We must change

Water feature in the Harnhill garden

direction from the relentless use of pesticides, herbicides, fungicides and antibiotics. We need to work with nature and not against it; we need to rethink our systems. Agriculture ought to be the primary health service of the nation. The old adage: 'You are what you eat' could go further: we are a product of our land; a healthy soil produces a healthy nation."

David Ursell's paper reminds me of a book I was lent about forty years ago called "Silent Spring" (Rachel Carson). The title was thought-provoking. The author argued that if we went on using pesticides the way we were it would not be long before our Springs would be silent of bird songs and our rivers empty of fish. The book was challenging, but I'm afraid my reaction was: "It's exaggerated, over the top." But in the years since, I have seen it's warnings fulfilled. On a stretch of the River Coln that I used to fish for trout, the water meadowlands were ploughed up for corn. Within a year or two it was noticeable the fish were smaller and fewer of them. The river vegetation changed, with less water shrimp and no crayfish. More recently during the last ten years in our Cotswold garden, the birds have almost disappeared; there is no longer a song thrush, warbler, wren or chaffinch. I have not heard a cuckoo for two years, presumably because of the lack of nests in which to lay its eggs.

In going over to New England U.S.A in the years since "Silent Spring" was written there, I have been glad to see and hear a goodly number of birds and have been impressed with the care of their rivers now. There is a policy to replenish the rivers with fish, not by restocking but by nurturing the wild fish and making suitable conditions for them. I was also impressed by the restraint of the fishermen in returning the fish to the water instead of taking them home to eat. The day that David Ursell spoke at the Harnhill Centre we had a double bill; James More-Molyneux was the other speaker.

James and Sue are a most charming and courageous couple. Among other things they led the way in organic products after the second world war. The story is told in a delightful book by James called "The Loseley Challenge." The name itself will be known to many by the yoghurt, ice-cream and other organic products of that name. We heard that day at Harnhill something of the hard work and challenge in getting these products off the ground and also something of their Christian faith which they needed. Speaking on faith James and Sue were most supportive of us in setting up the Centre at Harnhill, and have continued to be supportive and pray for us every day. They have now set up a Christian Cancer Help Centre at Loseley Park.

The driving force of James and Sue's lives is their Christian faith. I got to know them very well when they joined the third and last tour that I led In the Steps of Saint Francis in Italy in 1995. They, like myself, have a great admiration of Saint Francis and James is a member of the Third Order of Saint Francis. We talked together a good deal about him as we went round some of the special places in Francis' life. One day we went by coach from Assisi to one of my favourites, Greccio, a cave high up in the side of a mountain in the region of Rieti and overlooking a beautiful valley. It was a place where Francis loved to go for prayer and refreshment and the people in that area responded to him. We had a lovely outdoor communion service alongside the little cave monastery. It was in the cave that the concept of a Christmas Crib started. Francis was there one December and the day before Christmas Eve he asked a nearby farmer friend for the loan of a donkey and an ox. His followers took invitations out to the local people to come to the cave for Christmas Eve Midnight Mass which the local priest would celebrate (for Francis was never a priest). The valley and mountain side twinkled with lantern light as the people made their way there. In the cave amidst straw they saw an ox, an ass and a manger. Francis preached on the simplicity humility and poverty of Christ as illustrated by the manner of his birth. Simplicity, humility and poverty were three of the hallmarks of Francis and his followers. The other was obedience.

Francis sought to obey literally what Jesus taught and got his followers to do the same giving all they had to the poor including any donations given to them. They were to possess nothing but their rough brown robe, care for the underprivileged, the sick and especially the lepers, setting up a leprosarium just outside Assisi. When he sent them out he told them: "Preach the Gospel to all and use words if you must." They were to preach the Gospel by their example more than by their words, especially in their care for the poor, the sick and the lepers.

Another of his mountain retreats that we went to was a cave high up on Mount La Verna, given him by a local rich man who heard him preach. It was there during long hours and days of prayer and fasting that he received the 'Stigmata,' the wounds of Christ in his hands and side.

As well as the all importance of prayer to him was his great reverence for all of God's creation. Hence his speaking of brother sun and sister moon and mother earth, as recorded in his "Canticle to the Sun":

"O most high, almighty, good Lord God, to Thee belong praise, glory, honour and all blessing!

Praised be my Lord God with all his creatures, and especially our brother the sun who brings us the day and who brings us the light; fair is he who shines with a very great splendour; O Lord he signifies to us Thee.

Praised be my Lord for our sister the moon and for the stars, the which He has set clear and lovely in heaven.

Praised be my Lord for our brother the wind and for air and cloud, calms and all weathers, by which thou upholdest life in all creatures.

Praised be my Lord for our sister water, who is very serviceable unto us and humble and precious and clean.

Praised be my Lord for our brother fire through whom thou givest us light in the darkness; and he is bright and pleasant and very mighty and strong.

Praised be my Lord for our mother the earth, the which does sustain and keep us and bringest forth divers fruits and flowers of many colours and grass.

Praised be my Lord for all those who pardon one another for His love's sake and who endure weaknesses and tribulation; blessed are they who shall peaceably endure, for Thou O Most Highest, shall give them a crown.

Praised be my Lord for our sister the death of the body, from which no man escapeth. Woe to him who dieth in mortal sin!

Blessed are they who are found walking by Thy most holy will, for the second death shall have no power to harm them.

Praise ye and bless ye the Lord and give thanks unto Him and serve Him with great humility."

The love of Francis for all God's creation is for many seen in his love of birds and their love of him. It is reported that birds welcomed him wherever he went with cheerful song; so much so that on at least one occasion he had to ask the birds to be quiet for a time while he preached to the people. Then there is the well-known story of him preaching to the birds. Typical of his reverence of God's creation is his love for birds expressed in his words to them; "O little brother bird, that brimmest with full heart and having naught, possessed all, surely thou dost well to sing! For thou hast life without labour, and beauty without burden, and riches without care. When thou wakest lo, it is dawn; and thou comest to sleep it is eve and when thy two wings be folded about thy heart, lo there is rest. Therefore sing, Brother, having this great wealth that when thou singest thou givest thy riches to all."

During our Steps of Saint Francis tour another place we went to was the fascinating hill city of Gubbio. In ancient times the leaders of Gubbio had a great problem with a wolf that was ravaging their city. Francis by this time, was well known and they sent a message to Assisi begging him to come and help. He went and asked the details and then set off for the wolf's lair outside the city, while the citizens held back in fear. Francis found the wolf and talked to him telling him that he had been a naughty wolf, however if he would mend his ways he, Francis, would arrange for food to be left for each day at a certain place. Francis then returned to the city leaders and told them that they must arrange for food to be put each day at a certain place just outside the city. This they did and had no more trouble with the wolf and became fond of him and made him the city's mascot. And if anyone reckons that there are no wolves in Italy, let me disillusion them. When escaping during the last world war over the Apennines in Central Italy we came across two packs of wolves.

St. Francis and the Wolf

Francis, like Jesus before him, went aside for long periods of prayer and silent communion with the Heavenly Father. This was the source of his inspiration and power as it is for all great Christians. Mother Theresa, who is known world-wide for her care of the destitute and dying is not so well known for her disciplined prayer life. She has said: "We need to find God and He cannot be found in noise and restlessness. God is the friend of silence. See how nature – trees, flowers, grass – grows in silence. The more we receive in prayer the more we can give in the active life.' As Francis de Sales said two centuries ago: "Every Christian needs at least half an hour of quiet prayer and bible reading first thing every morning; except when he has a very busy day ahead of him; then he needs a full hour!"

Francis' life of extreme simplicity, poverty, obedience, prayer and reverence for all God's creation was such a challenging example that his movement spread across Europe while he was still alive, bringing cleansing to a lax church and change to an immoral society.

The bravery and commitment, hard work and prayer of James and Sue, David and Susan, has been an example to others. Organic food gets ever more prominent even on the shelves of our supermarkets but pesticides and the like are only one aspect of the present malaise of our world as David hinted in his paper. Genetics and genetic engineering almost weekly seem to explore new fields of life on earth. There is the increasing threat of global warming and climate change, while some rich nations refuse to diminish their pollution because it would reduce their finances. There are no doubt other things that threaten the created life on our planet. I am not a scientist or a politician but as a Christian I can say, "Reverence God's creation or we perish."

We are fortunate that there are places in the world where we can get a glimpse of God's creation as it is meant to be. We saw some as we visited the retreats of Saint Francis in Italy. I am writing this in another. I am in Marcia Gibson-Watt's studio above their garage at their home seven miles from Builth Wells. Each large window looks out over the most beautiful unspoilt rural countryside with sheep quietly grazing.

Guests who come to the Harnhill Centre often remark upon how they feel wrapped round in God's love. The peace and beauty of the place are entirely due to the loving care and attention of the staff and the presence of Jesus. The beauty is in part due to the lovely garden looked after by volunteers, not least Theresa Vearncombe, who has organised the volunteers over a number of years. Theresa told me of one guest in her late fifties. On arriving for the first time she saw the shrubbery around the new wing and said to herself: "Oh great, they have a garden!" As she walked toward the house she noticed some weeds among the plants and said to herself: "I will be happy here." When the guest told her the next day Theresa said: "Praise the Lord!." Her vision was that the garden should be beautiful but not clinically tidy, so that the guests should feel comfortable. That goes for inside the house which aims to be homely and non threatening. The parklands surrounding the garden in which sheep quietly graze add to the sense of peace.

"Uzziah built towers in the desert land and dug many cisterns. He had people working in his fields and vineyards in the hills and the fertile lands for he loved the soil" (2 Chron 26v10). Too few of our leaders today love the soil. They are dismissive about what is happening to our agriculture and rural communities, presumably because they represent fewer votes than urban communities. There is a great need for leaders who, with inspiration and determination, will reverse the process of the desecration of our countryside.

There are some people who give themselves unstintingly to help the disadvantaged and the marginalised.

Over the years at Harnhill we have had many excellent speakers. One of the most brilliant was James Odgers. His subject was related to this present chapter namely "Healing the community." James has already had a most interesting life though still youngish with young children. He has been a successful London solicitor and banker. He and his wife worked with Jackie Pullenger for six months and also went round many of the poorest and disadvantaged communities in the world. He has now set up the Besom Foundation which is intensely practical. He matches what people have to give to an appropriate need. This may be a large sum of money all of which will be used in a way the donor approves or the giving can concern small practical things like volunteers (mainly young Christians) collecting the soap used for only one night in a well known London hotel and taking it to a down-and-out hostel. Similarly shoes that a well known shop is moving off its shelves because they are out of fashion are distributed to those in need.

Besom often get small projects started in areas of poverty and unemployment. One such project helped start a silk worm factory in a poor country which employs a number of women whose only income otherwise would have been from prostitution. James works closely with the Social Services and the story of Maria illustrates just the kind of practical work that Besom does.

Maria escaped domestic violence and was left with virtually nothing. She tells how a little help and a little time has given her a leg-up and the chance to make a new start:

"My social worker told me about the Besom and I agreed to let them help me – even though that was hard for me. Sarah (Volunteering Department) introduced me to the leaders of the volunteers who were going to paint my flat and it was to be over two Saturdays. It was the first time I had ever entrusted my keys to anyone."

"The first Saturday with all the painting they did, it looked very messy but I thought 'Don't worry, next Saturday the flat will look much better!' The next Saturday I went out with my kids and when I came back, I was so excited. The house looked lovely. I chose the colours beforehand and they did it the way I wanted. My daughters were so pleased with the changes. I began to talk to Sophie (Recycling Department) about beds and a few things for us – even the colours we wanted. Like God is with you. Something like that. I was very surprised. I got more in two months than I did in ten years. The nicest thing is to see the smiling face of my eldest and to see her happy again.

I wished for a miracle and since arriving here, it has happened. I feel I can pick up my life again."

These charities seem to be small against the many great problems and needs. But they are beginning to grow rapidly each year. Saint Francis began in a very small way in a small place, but his influence was felt across Europe in thirty years,

It is to the Christian we must look for the restoration of society to the standard that Christ desires for it . The first twelve apostles had deeply influenced the whole Roman Empire within less than a hundred years by their sheer quality of life. A letter to Diagnetus, probably in the second century, to explain the Christian faith, says:

"These Christians know and trust God. They placate those who oppress them, make them their friends, they do good to their enemies. Their wives are absolutely pure and their daughters modest. Their men abstain from all unlawful marriage and from all impurity. If they see a stranger they take him into their dwellings and rejoice over him as a real brother. Oh how these Christians love one another, truly it is a new people and there is something divine about them."

It was Jesus who demonstrated that the only way to heal and restore those four broken relationships was through unselfish sacrificial love. Those early Christians, like Saint Francis later, continued bringing healing and restoration through the same way: unselfish sacrificial love.

Many outstanding intellectuals who have struggled with great philosophical and theological issues have come to the same conclusion, namely that the most powerful and effective force in life is gentle but strong love, confirming Saint Paul's conclusion in 1 Cor. 13v13.

Baron von Hügel the great intellectual divine of the 19th century said on his death bed to his niece who was looking after him: "the greatest thing in heaven and earth is love."

Karl Barth, the great theologian of the 20th century, at the end of thousands of pages in his Church Dogmatics, arrived at this simple definition of God; "The one who loves." Some years later someone asked him what was his main conclusion after all his theological studies. He replied: "Jesus loves me, this I know, for the Bible tells me so."

Harvest

November 6th 1999 was a great day in the life of the Harnhill Centre of Christian Healing. It was the celebration and dedication of the restored barn by the Bishop of Chelmsford, the Rt Rev John Perry.

This lovely old Harvest Barn, in the first year of the Centre's life had been hastily cleared and whitewashed in a couple of days by a few volunteers led by David Ursell. The need to use it had become very urgent in view of the increasing numbers of people coming to the Wednesday evening healing service and Saturday teaching courses. The cleaned-up Barn served us well in spite of the odd cobweb and occasional droppings from above and a less than salubrious entrance through the old chemical store. Now we have this beautiful large auditorium, pristinely decorated and lit, high and lofty exposing the wonderful old beams. The whole place radiates glory, the shekinah glory of the Old Testament indicating the radiant presence of God. A most suitable place for the Harvest of restored lives.

A young man I had known well over forty years ago and who had become a Baptist minister, came to stay at Harnhill a year before the celebration and dedication. He learned of the plans to renovate the barn. He said to me: "Will that complete your original vision for the Centre?" I replied, "As far as the buildings are concerned, yes! But there is a long way to go to complete the whole vision. That will not be completed until all peoples' needs have been met in Christ and their lives completely renewed." I might have said, "Not until all the four broken relationships from the Fall have been completely healed."

A few years before the work on the Barn had started, Letty, my wife, had a vision or a picture which she did not tell me about until some time after the Barn was renovated. In it she saw long queues of people looking dishevelled, unhappy and bowed down filing into the front entrance of the Barn. Out of the side exit were coming streams of people, upright, joyful, radiant and without their burdens.

Another vision by way of a dream, was given to Judith in her home twenty miles away. She knew Harnhill and comes from time to time but did not know of the plan to renovate the Barn. She wrote down her dream at the time not knowing what it was about. Here it is:

"We are standing outside an old barn, walls of stone speaking of times and events long past, familiar in its setting. The entrance is low, the wooden door stands ajar waiting expectantly. It seems that all is dark inside, and silent."

"I have just come out from inside the barn. I know that despite the sense of silence and darkness, there is a shelter here. Inside, long tables are set out; a banquet is being prepared."

"Around the door a crowd has gathered. Some look in through the entrance, they are anxious and unsure. The barn is dark, its ceiling rafters are rough and bare, dusty cobwebs float in the light cast by the open door. The tables are not decorated, there is an uncertain air."

"I am anxious that the barn is not ready, worried that the people will not want to come in as there is still much that needs finishing to make this place comfortable and welcoming. I am excited that this is God's plan and it's going to be good – if we can reassure and encourage the people."

"The crowd is growing as more people arrive. They approach the doorway with interest but somewhat apprehensively. I begin to encourage them to cross the threshold and a number decide to come in and bending low, they enter as others follow."

"The time of indecision has passed and I must not pause any longer but press on, turning back only to those eager ones with words of kindness and encouragement."

"We weave between chairs and tables, more people spread out, the movement reverberating through the stillness. A fine dust begins to filter down through the space from the rafters, so the further into the barn we go, the thicker the shower from above becomes until the people begin to falter, discouraged by this unpleasant distraction. I am spurred on by the urgency of the need to persuade the people not to turn back or give up. This disturbance is an inevitable consequence of our presence, we must move on."

"I too, though, seem overcome by anxiety and wake from the dream but just at that moment, I sense the light, right in the far corner of the barn and I glimpse a winding stair. I realise the light is coming from above the ceiling. This is the reason we need to move on to reach the light, the truth is that the rafters of this ceiling are not meant to remain any longer. Above is the glorious roof of strong timber, giving shelter, with its beauty in light and space. The promise of what is to be, of what is good and strong and light and true is real. It will happen! don't be afraid."

"I have seen this barn, walls of Cotswold stone familiar in its setting, expectant and waiting low rafters, rough and bare."

"Through worship, love and steadfast faith, encouragement and hope it becomes that shelter and banqueting hall with its glorious roof of strong timber beautiful in light and space – for God knew it would be so."

"May this barn stand as a sign of the Kingdom with its message of hope, a sign of the grace of God who makes his strength perfect in our weakness, a sign of the church growing through struggles to healing and wholeness, a sign for you. 'Speak Lord, your servant is listening.'"

Judith did not connect this dream with Harnhill until some months later when she saw the restored Barn for the first time. Then she knew it was Harnhill. Up to then she thought it might refer to her local church or to the Church in general. Of course it could refer to the Church in general as well as the Barn at Harnhill.

Bishop John Perry's sermon in the service of celebration for the restored Barn spoke of Harnhill as a place of Hope, Healing, Humour and Happiness.

"Hope is the heart of the Gospel' said the Bishop. "Our society needs such places of hope where the people can come."

"Healing. Where there is hope there is healing" commented Bishop John. He spoke of the importance of forgiveness because forgiveness heals.

"Humour. Good health is a laughing matter" and spoke of the need of humour in a society where each person is valued for who they are. Proverbs 17v22: "A cheerful heart is good medicine."

"Happiness. Harnhill is a foretaste of Heaven." Said Bishop Perry. He went on to say that Heaven is not a geographical location in time and space. It is a permanent celebration where a handicapped grandchild is now able to run and dance and give praise.

Bishop John took as his text the parable of the mustard seed. Harnhill was born out of the small seed of an idea. The mustard seed grew into a tree and the birds of the air nested in it. Like the seed in the parable, the Centre had grown into a tree, a tree with many branches so that there was plenty of room for God's people to come and meet with Him there. The branches were not to be stiff but yielding to meet the varying need of those who come to Harnhill, a place of hope, healing, humour and a taste of Heaven.

When Jesus was about to send out the seventy-two he said to them: "The harvest is plentiful, but the labourers are few; pray therefore the Lord of the harvest to send out labourers into the harvest." (Luke 10v2) One of the objectives of Harnhill is not only to encourage people to come to Jesus to be healed of their hurts and any of the four broken relationships we have mentioned. but also to receive the fullness of the Holy Spirit to equip them with gifts and fruit to enable them also to be labourers in God's harvest. We have training days and courses to this end.

Tessa, part of whose story is at the beginning of this book, through the filling of the Holy Spirit began to experience the gifts of the Spirit including messages of knowledge, wisdom and prophecy. She writes:

"A few years ago I shared a message of great encouragement from the Lord publicly at Harnhill. The sharing took enormous courage on my part but the impact of the words was such that copies were made in the office for people to take home with them. So many felt that the word was absolutely right for them personally at that time. One woman said to me, with a radiant smile on her face and tears pouring down her cheeks, 'this is the answer I have been praying for!' Another lady asked me for permission to send it to another church fellowship and have it printed in her parish magazine! What had been given as a deeply personal message became, with its sharing, one of universal joy and hope. And so I share it again, even more widely praying that it will touch the hearts of all who are in need of its message: 'My child, you may feel yourself sometimes far from me, but fear not that I am far from you. I am ever with you, to each side of you to comfort you, before you to guide you, behind you to protect you, within you to nourish you and sustain you. Take your fill of Me at each and every moment. It is My delight to fill you with My joy – to have you aware of Me so that together we may share of God's great and bounteous love.'

Christine found it hard to believe that an ordinary lay person like herself could be used in the churche's ministry. She thought that only 'special' people would hear God speaking. After training at Harnhill she and her husband are regular members of the prayer ministry team and Christine regularly receives messages from God. In the preparation time before a healing service when the team wait on the Lord for any words or pictures, a picture of a Japanese flag appeared in her mind. Christine says: "It was so odd I had to speak it out, albeit reluctantly. The picture was given out together with other words in the service." Christine says, "To my amazement the first person who came up to us for prayer ministry said, 'The Japanese flag spoke to me.' I was so surprised I asked the person to say why. 'I'm a missionary on leave from Japan and this is the first time I have been to Harnhill,' she replied." What a blessing for her to know God knew exactly where she was and what she wanted. God brought us into contact again more than once, and we now support her in prayer in her work as a missionary in Sapporo, Japan.

It is often the more unusual pictures or words received in the preparation time before a service that bring a response. Pam had a picture of someone pushing a wheelbarrow absolutely full of very pungent manure. This picture along with others was given out in the service by the leader. "During the prayer ministry a girl whom we never met before came straight up to us," says Pam. "The girl said, 'If it is a barrow full of manure it must be for me.' Some time later the girl requested counselling." The co-ordinator sent the request to Pam and her husband, without knowing they already knew her, and she has been going to them regularly and Jesus has been meeting her many deep needs and doing wonders in her life, making her a new person.

God the Holy Spirit really is in charge. He gives a funny picture to Pam. An unknown person responds and goes to the very person who had the picture rather than to any of the other twelve couples ministering at the service. The co-ordinator then sends the request for counselling to Pam and John rather than to any other of the thirty or forty counsellors.

For a harvest, the labourers must keep Jesus central in their lives and be completely dependent upon the Holy Spirit to empower, equip and guide them. Human endeavour, techniques, methods may help but only Jesus is the healer and the Holy Spirit is the enabler through his gifts and fruit. We can do nothing for salvation in our own strength.

John Mockett, the Deputy Warden of Harnhill put something of this truth in an amusing piece of writing:

"Jesus went through all the towns and villages, teaching ....preaching.... and healing .... When He saw the crowds, He had compassion on them, because they were harassed and helpless, like sheep without a shepherd. Then He said to His disciples, "The harvest is plentiful but the workers are few. Ask the Lord of the harvest therefore, to send out workers into His harvest field. (Matthew 9: 35 to 38)

"Dear Lord of the harvest please will you send out workers into your harvest field."

"Great, John, when can you start?'

"No Lord you've got me wrong, I've just been told to ask you!"

"Well you'll do just fine. Just the sort of chap I've been looking for, I can really use you."

"What, me, really? Well yes that's great, I'll just go and grab my coat and I'll be off."

"Um John, where are you going?'

"Well, the harvest field, you said you could really use me."

"Yes I can and will, but I don't want you to go alone."

"You mean Pete can come too? Well that's brilliant, I'll go and find him"

"John, Pete may come as well but I was thinking of me going with you, if that's OK with you?"

"OK? I should say so, that's even better, I'll just sit here and read the paper and you can give me the nod when you're ready"

"John, why don't you walk around with me while I get things ready and you might pick up one or two tips. What do you say?"

"Terrific, where do we start?"

Some time later:

"Well John how are things going, everything alright?"

"Lord it's just brilliant being with you all the time, seeing how you do things and listening to what you are saying, but I am a bit worried about these sorts of growths that I've noticed appearing on me over the last little while"

"Oh! Those are the fruits of my spirit, nothing to worry about at all. Look there's some love and this one's joy and over here is a bit of patience growing. Oh! And some peace as well. My Spirit has been busy during our time together."

"I can't believe it, me having all these fruits and more besides. I'll look forward to eating those when they're ripe."

"No John! They are not for you, but for you to share with others so that they can come and join us too. That fruit you are bearing is a part of the harvest and the more time you spend with me the more fruit you will bear, but if you try and do things on your own, well, the fruit won't grow."

"I see Lord! Well I don't really, but I believe you. Lord would you give me a nudge if I start drifting off 'cos there are lots of people I can think of who could do with having a chat with you and if part of that means them feeding off your fruit in me then I need to stick close."

"I am the vine; you are the branches. If a man remains in me and I in him, he will bear much fruit, apart from me you can do nothing" (John. 15v5) "

Although on the farms of old we were apt to think of the harvest at a particular time of year, say August and September, in fact harvesting goes on through much of the year especially in other countries. Even here the harvesting of the various crops is almost continuous with sugar beet, lambs, calves, pigs, grasses, soft fruit, winter corn, spring corn, other cereals, hard fruit, kale, sprouts and other greens.

So with the spiritual harvest at Harnhill; it goes on the whole year. But there is always the final harvest to come when all will be safely gathered in! As one of the old hymns says: "All the world is God's own field, crops unto His praise to yield;" but it goes on to talk of the final harvest when all will be gathered in to God's own barn.

The Harvest Barn at Harnhill

In the End God

The world is not going to peter out or be ended by man in either a whimper or a bang. It will be ended by God.

In the beginning God and in the end God, and all in between belongs to God, however much man may vainly try to wrest it from Him. And the end is going to be glorious and triumphant.

Agnostics and atheists do not know where they are going or what is their end. Christians do know and it is glorious and triumphant. Many times Jesus promised He was coming back again and Jesus always keeps His promises. Strangely, although many Christians talk enthusiastically about Jesus' first visit to Earth, not so many get excited about this planned return visit.

Sometimes when I have led retreats I have taken for my four talks the subject of four gardens. Most people love gardens even if they are not so keen on gardening. It is a subject with which they can easily identify and on first appearance does not seem to be heavily theological.

The first garden is the Garden of Eden which we have already considered. A garden of perfection and beauty the like of which has not been equalled. It was also blessed with the companionship of God. A garden in which God was in the habit of walking and talking in relaxed communion with the inhabitants in the cool of the evening. The despoiling of that perfection and harmony and its planned restoration have been the subject of this book.

The second garden is Gethsemane. It is a very special place especially for those who know it physically, with its very ancient gnarled olive trees and the great flat slab of rock upon which Jesus is thought to have thrown Himself in prayer. But it is even more special for all who know its spiritual significance for mankind's salvation as Jesus wrestled out in agonising prayer the costly way forward. As the well-known hymn puts it: "And in the garden secretly, and on the Cross on high, should strive afresh against the foe: should strive and should prevail."

The third one is the garden of the resurrection which proclaims the victory won in the previous garden. Although the site in the Crusaders' Church is probably the historical position of the resurrection, General Gordon's Garden Tomb brings one aesthetically closer to the triumphant event. We have had some very moving celebrations of Holy Communion in that garden against its backdrop of the empty tomb. On my first visits, there was a wonderful old Christian Arab gardener. Seeing him it was easy to imagine the gardener Mary Magdalene thought she saw that first Easter morning. It is a very precious place.

The fourth garden is also very precious: paradise. Jesus said to the penitent thief: " Today you will be with me in paradise" (Luke. 23v43). Paradise is an ancient Persian word for a walled pleasure garden. Such gardens in hot desert countries were very special. Coming out of the hot, dusty and smelly streets into a garden was pure joy. The colourful scented flowers, the soft green of shrubs and grass, the running water, were so refreshing and renewing. One of the highest honours a king of those countries in those days could bestow upon a citizen was to make him a Companion of the Garden. This meant that the honoured citizen had permission to enter the king's garden whenever he wished to enjoy it. That pleasure was even greater if the king came in the cool of the evening to walk and talk with the citizen. Such will be the ecstasy of Christians in the Kingdom of Heaven. Paradise symbolises the state to which God and man are restored to the perfect fellowship that existed before sin entered the world (Rev. 2v7).

Meanwhile we are on Earth where men and women continue to seek the meaning and purpose of life on this planet.

Sir Arnold Toynbee in his many-volumed "A Study of History," was led to believe that "Religion is the most important thing in life .... History seen solely from the standpoint of each human participant in it is a tale told by an idiot signifying nothing. But this apparently senseless 'sound of fury' acquires meaning when man catches in history a glimpse of the operation of the One True God .... Man's fragmentary and ephemeral participation in territorial history is indeed redeemed for him when he can play his part as the voluntary co-adjutor of a God whose mastery of the situation gives a divine value and meaning to man's otherwise paltry endeavours."

Another historian, Herbert Butterfield, former Professor of Modern History at Cambridge, takes a similar view. He believes that history testifies to Christianity and that Christianity interprets history. In his book "Christianity and History," published in 1949, he concludes that Christ is the firm Rock at the Centre of History. A Rock that historical events cannot shake, nor can they shake us if we hold to Christ the Rock. In chapter five: "Providence in the Historical Process," he writes: "We might say that this human story is like a piece of orchestral music that we are playing over for the first time. As the second clarinet I never know what is coming after the page that now lies before me. If I am sure that B flat is the next note I have to play, I can never feel certain that it will not come with surprising implications until I have heard what the other people are going to play at the same moment. And no single person in the orchestra can have any idea when or where this piece of music is going to end." He goes on: "To make the comparison authentic we must imagine the composer himself is only composing the music inch by inch as the orchestra is playing it." So that if you or I are playing a wrong note he changes his mind and says to himself: "We can only straighten out that piece of untidiness if we pass for a moment from the major into the minor key."

I would add that the composer does have clear in his mind what he is creating and how it will end.

Another writer likened life on earth to creating a huge tapestry with each of us putting a particular piece of wool into it. We are doing so from the back of the tapestry and the appearance is messy and bitty and our vision limited to the part around which we are working. It doesn't look too attractive. Only after death and when all have made their contribution will we be able to see the whole design and its full beauty from the front of the tapestry.

To Peter we are living stones being built into a spiritual house with Jesus as the chief corner stone or capstone (1 Peter. 2v5).

Jesus speaks of himself as the vine and each of us as branches. It is essential for us to abide in the vine if we are to bear fruit which is His purpose for us (John 15v1-8). Paul calls the church the Body of Christ. Each of us is a member or limb. Each limb is important and indispensable. If one suffers all suffer (1 Cor. 12v12-26).

Judith Maltby, chaplain and fellow of All Souls Oxford comments on the purpose of this body. She recently said: "If you take the Christian claim seriously, that history has as it ultimate goal the reconciliation of creation with the Creator .... then the institutional church .... is a body to promote that purpose." By implication each of us together with other Christians have a part to play in these purposes. As the Warden of Harnhill has said: "We're in the restoration business! That goes for all Christians."

Paul has quite a lot to say about the last days when he writes to the Thessalonians but he also urges them to work. It would seem as if they were downing tools and idly waiting because they anticipated the Lord's return at any moment. Even if His return is imminent there is plenty of work for the Christian. Matthew 24v14 says: "The gospel of the Kingdom will be preached throughout the whole world .... and then the end will come." I like to think that preaching the gospel not only means speaking it but applying it by healing the sick, feeding the hungry and restoring broken relationships. It can mean sitting quietly alongside someone at home or in hospital in deepest depression compounded by guilt and shame and listening if and when the person speaks. Then when the opportunity comes, quietly encouraging him or her by sharing the gospel truths of the forgiveness and love of Jesus who regards the sick person as special and precious. He or she may well not be able to take it in the first time, but after gently repeating these truths with conviction the penny will suddenly drop and another soul has been won for God's harvest.

What of the end? It includes the Second coming of Christ in Glory but it also includes a great deal else. Many places in the Bible relate apocalyptic events preceding the end. Jesus tells us of them in Mark 13, Matthew 24 and Luke 21. There are many more details in the Book of Revelation. These passages have led to detailed interpretation through the centuries.

With great imagination and application the authors Tim Lahaye and Jerry B Jenkins have written a series of exciting novels seeking to apply the details of these apocalyptic passages to our present day. They include "Left Behind," "Tribulation Force" and "Soul Harvest."

In each generation some people have confidently predicted the end on a certain day in a certain year at a particular time. When that time has come and gone they have had to revise their ideas. It is certainly not difficult today to find all the events and signs that Jesus mentions happening before the end. It behoves us to be on the alert and watch as Jesus tells us to but also to note that He goes on to say: "Of that day and that hour we know not, not even the angels in heaven nor the Son, but only the Father. Take heed, watch, for you do not know when the time will come." (Mark 13v22-33). Rather than speculate, we "live each day as if the last" as the hymn puts it and get on with the restoration business.

And what of the end? After the last things what of Christ's final coming? Paul and the writer of the Revelation tells us that He comes to receive His Bride the Church (i.e. all Christians), to take her to the Marriage Feast. A bride goes through a great deal of preparation for her wedding. At one of the more recent marriages I have taken the prospective bride turned up at the church for the rehearsal extremely casually dressed in grubby jeans and jumper with her hair all over the place. She was really scruffy. The next time I saw her a few days later, I had a great deal of difficulty in believing she was the same girl; radiantly beautiful, most elegantly dressed, sparklingly clean all ready for her bridegroom and marriage. The Church, Christ's Bride today resembles the first picture rather than the second. Fortunately when Christ sees the first picture, He also sees the potential: the second. But there is still a great deal of preparation. We pray for the cleaning purifying work of the Holy Spirit for all of us so that we may be "a radiant church without stain or wrinkles or any other blemish, but holy and blameless." (Ephesians 5v27).

People speculate a great deal about heaven and what it will be like. The book of Revelation speaks of a Holy City with specific details including measurements, the decoration of precious stones and the streets of pure gold. We have already mentioned the garden of paradise and the bride and her wedding feast. C. S. Lewis wrote a delightful book called "The Great Divorce" in which there are a few surprises.

Jesus speaks about the quality of life in the Kingdom of Heaven sometimes through parables. In one place towards the end of his earthly life He tells the disciples quite plainly "I go to prepare a place for you .... that where I am you may be also." He says in John 14v2 "in my Father's house there are many resting places (or mansions)."

The late William Temple points out that the word translated "resting places" is the word for "caravanserais." On one of my early parties I led to the Holy Land we went to Acre in the North. After seeing a church there the guide took a short cut to get us back to the coach by the harbour. Our route took us through the centre of the old city and we suddenly found ourselves in a large empty square or rather oblong. At one end there was a solid gate, at the other end a small door through which we had come, otherwise it was completely closed. Stephen, a historian headmaster of a grammar school, said excitedly: "What a wonderful ancient caravanserai!" and he quoted John 14v2: "In my Father's house are many caravanserais." All round the sides were rows of pillars and the space between the pillars an open room or resting place. The pillars supported a walkway all around and a series of lock-up rooms, one above each resting place. In the centre of the square was a drinking fountain and trough. So when a caravan of camels came across the hot dusty desert to the walled city of Acre and entered it, they proceeded to the caravanserai. Once inside each merchant or traveller went to a vacant resting place and unloaded any precious merchandise or possessions straight from the camel's back on to the gallery platform to be put into the lock up room. Then the camels and their travellers could be watered from the fountains and no doubt local merchants were on hand to sell food and fodder.

The facilities of the caravanserai may indicate some of the features of heaven. Here there was great security within the inner walls as well as the outer walls of the city. Here was rest for weary travellers as well as water and food and fellowship to refresh them. Elsewhere Jesus promises those who are weary and heavy laden if they come to Him will have rest and refreshment (Matt. 11v28). Heaven is coming to Jesus, life with Jesus, that is the main thing we need to know about heaven, life with Him forever. Eternal life, of which the New Testament speaks a great deal, is not just everlasting life, it is a vibrant, pure, holy quality of divine life. That we should have it is the purpose for which Jesus came and died and rose again: "God so loved the world that he gave His one and only Son, that whoever believes in Him shall not perish but have eternal life." (John 3v16).

Life is certainly one of the essential characteristics of the Kingdom of Heaven, eternal life. Jesus tells us very little about the activities of Heaven: He does speak of banquets and worship but has more to say about the characteristics and quality of those people in the Kingdom of Heaven now and hereafter. Vibrant life is one characteristic ; "I came that they might have life and have it abundantly." (John 10v10).

Joy is another characteristic: "that my joy may be in you and that your joy may be full (or complete)" (John 15v11). Not a surface frothy happiness but a deep permanent joy.

The peace that Jesus gives is also a deep inner peace, not just the absence of noise or problems: "Peace I leave with you, my peace I give to you; not as the world gives do I give to you. Let not you heart be troubled neither let it be afraid." (John 14v27). After the resurrection Jesus comes to the frightened disciples through locked doors and says to them: "Peace be with you" and having shown them his pierced hands and side says again: "Peace be with you. As the Father sent me, even so I send you." (John 20v19-21).

Another great characteristic of the Kingdom of Heaven is another fruit of the Spirit, love. This is a quality central to the Christian life here and hereafter just as it is a central characteristic of God revealed in Christ. Christians have not been given books of rules and instructions by Jesus but told to love: love God with all heart, soul, mind and strength and love others as themselves.

Glory is another particular characteristic of heaven and of God. In the Old Testament glory signifies the presence of God and is awesome and even frightening. Glory is also frequently spoken of in the New Testament and is awesome but not so frightening. Jesus manifests God's glory in His signs and miracles of love. (John 2v11).

Glory is the particular attribute of God and of heaven. In John 17v5 Jesus prays:

"Father glorify me in your presence with the glory I had with you before the world began." That glory Jesus relinquished when He Himself became a human baby in a manger. Jesus is about to return to heaven and asks His Father to be given back the glory now His work on earth is finished (John 17v4). During His work on earth Jesus has shown that the awesome glory of God is full of love. As the late William Temple wrote: "If God is love, His glory most of all shines forth in whatever most fully expresses love. The Cross of shame is the Throne of Glory. The sacrifice and humiliation are the divine glory." And in his gospel John speaks of the Cross and resurrection of Jesus as glorification (John 7v39).

Although glory may be a particular attribute of God and of heaven, yet at times we may catch a glimpse of it here, maybe in a beautiful sunset or a magnificent view from the top of a mountain. Maybe in a symphony or great piece of music or in worship. At times in good worship it is possible to be carried out of the things of this world and caught up in the love and presence of God. Christian drama can do the same, especially through music. A few years ago I saw a musical in Cheltenham Town Hall: "Mary Magdalene" by Roger Jones whom we are fortunate to have at Harnhill occasionally. The story was told so sensitively in song, of Mary coming to realise that Jesus deeply loved her, sinful and worthless as she felt. He loved her for herself alone and not for what He could get from her as did other men. As this truth dawned on her she responded in deep intimate adoration and love in return. It brought home to me in a new way that God similarly loved me unworthy as I was. I wept copiously, more than ever before or since, I was not unhappy, rather the reverse. I was joyously caught up in the incredible love and presence of Jesus. It was a taste of the glory we shall enjoy fully and permanently in heaven.

The qualities of the Kingdom of heaven which Christians experience in part here on earth, will be enjoyed fully in heaven. Satan will have been vanquished and slain. The four broken relationships from the Fall completely restored and so there is no bar to our intimate union with God but perfect harmony again between the Creator and His creation as all join in with the heavenly song, "Holy, holy, holy, is the Lord God Almighty, who was and is and is to come" (Rev. 4v8). In the presence of Jesus we shall enjoy full vibrant eternal life, permanent joy, perfect peace, pure love and of course, glory. In Heaven there is no need of sun and moon as the glory supplies ample light (Rev 21v23).

"The harvest is the end of the age" (Matt. 13v39). After the sifting and the judgement and all Christian souls have been gathered into God's glorious great Harvest Barn, then the celebrations can begin the marriage feast of the Lamb and the Bride with glorious worship and full fellowship with each other and with God.

In the beginning God and in the end God.

The resident staff at Harnhill in AD 2000

In 1986 Harnhill Manor became the Harnhill Centre of Christian Healing as recounted in my previous book *Desert Harvest*.

Situated three miles east of Cirencester, the Centre has accommodation for up to twenty guests in comfortable twin bedded and single rooms. The adjacent barn complex includes a Conference Centre and a Counselling Wing. Alongside the Manor is a small Norman Church, which is available for visitors' use. A large well-kept garden encourages peace and tranquility and, together with the surrounding farmland, the country lanes provide ample opportunity for interesting Cotswold walks.

The programme includes short residential stays during which prayer counselling is normally available, training days on subjects related to Christian healing, two healing services a week on Wednesday 7.30pm and on Friday 10.30 am. Individual prayer counselling is available by appointment and requests for intercessory prayer are accepted for those unable to come to the Centre.

The present Warden, the Rev'd Paul Springate, soon after he arrived in 1997 was asked what his vision was for the future. He replied "I envisage a Centre where the worship, teaching and ministry, along with everyday activities of the house are so saturated in the love of God, that to come here is to meet Jesus powerfully through his Holy Spirit and where He is so present that healing comes just from being here and worshipping Him."

All enquiries and requests for further copies of *God's Harvest* or *Desert Harvest,* should be addressed to: –

The Secretary, Harnhill Manor, Cirencester, Glos, GL7 5PX

Tel: 01285 850283/4   Fax: 01285850519

E.mail: office@harnhillcentre.freeserve.co.uk

Website: www.harnhillcentre.freeserve.co.uk

Charity Registration Number: 292173

Arthur Dodds' new book: *God's Harvest*

God is in the restoration business. Since the Fall, when the creation relationship between man and his God, man and himself, man and his fellows and man and his environment was broken, God has been calling his people to come to him for restoration and healing.

In this long-awaited sequel to *Desert Harvest,* Canon Arthur Dodds opens with the restoration of the barn at the Harnhill Centre of Christian Healing. Once a storehouse for God's bounty, the harvest now being gathered in is of lives changed and healed, restored and forgiven as God's wonderful rescue plan is worked out through Jesus.

Many who come to Harnhill for help carry with them the pain of broken relationships and here they tell their stories, arriving in despair and leaving with hope for the future as they experience God's infinite love and compassion. —But this book is more than an encouraging testimony to God's grace; it also tells His-story – the amazing story of God's plans to restore mankind to wholeness.

In *God's Harvest,* Canon Dodds takes us on an exciting romp through the Bible. This story of God's unfolding purposes for mankind, told with clarity and simplicity that is at once easy to understand yet awesome in its majesty, brings the Bible alive and leaves no room for doubt that it is relevant today. Canon Dodds speaks convincingly yet gently of God's life-changing power as He meets us at the point of our need and gathers in His harvest. Inspiring, thrilling and lively, this story will encourage you on your journey with God.

Also, still in print, Arthur Dodds' other book: *Desert Harvest,* paperback, £5.90. Both books available from:

The Secretary, Harnhill Manor, Cirencester, Glos, GL7 5PX

Tel: 01285 850283/4 Fax: 01285850519

E.mail: office@harnhillcentre.freeserve.co.uk